THE
LULL-A-BABY
SLEEP PLAN

THE LULL-A-BABY SLEEP PLAN

THE SOOTHING, SUPERFAST WAY TO HELP YOUR NEW BABY SLEEP THROUGH THE NIGHT . . . AND PREVENT SLEEP PROBLEMS BEFORE THEY DEVELOP

CATHRYN TOBIN, MD

RODALE

ADVANCE PRAISE FOR
THE LULL-A-BABY SLEEP PLAN

BY CATHRYN TOBIN, MD

"Finally, a research-based solution to the age-old problem of getting Baby to sleep! Drawing on her extensive knowledge of infant neurological development as well as her years of experience as a practicing pediatrician, Dr. Tobin has created an approach that is simple, effective—and compassionate. *The Lull-a-Baby Sleep Plan* is not about letting babies cry; it's about understanding the sometimes counterintuitive conditions that help babies fall asleep on their own. This book should be required reading for all new parents!"

—*Linda Acredolo, PhD, co-author of the best-selling*
Baby Signs, Baby Minds, and Baby Hearts

"Parenting is a 24/7 job, and it can get pretty lonely at 3 AM, especially if you're the kind of parent who can't bear to let your child cry himself to sleep. That's why the Lull-a-Baby Sleep Plan is so wonderful. Dr. Cathryn Tobin not only has a gentle, caring approach to your baby but also has great empathy for what you're going through. New parents can help their infant learn healthy sleep habits from the get-go, and those who've missed the early window of opportunity can backtrack and solve bedtime battles with an older child. Drawing on her years of experience as a midwife, a pediatrician and a mom, Dr. Tobin illustrates her techniques with a wide variety of sleep problems. This is one book that should be in every parent's library."

—*Mary Mohler, editor-at-large,* Parents *magazine*

"Cathryn Tobin gives new parents the encouragement and inspiration to develop the skills they need to help their children sleep. Anyone who has struggled to put a child to bed night after night will appreciate the honest, direct, and practical approach Tobin uses. As a parent of four children and senior editor at *ePregnancy*, I know that sleep is one of the toughest issues new parents face. Kudos for a terrific road map to a good night's sleep for all kids—and their parents."

— *Julia Rosien, senior editor,* ePregnancy *magazine*

"Dr. Tobin's important and highly readable book offers parents medically sound and scientifically based sleep strategies that are attuned to the needs of both babies *and* parents. By teaching parents how to activate their baby's relaxation response, Dr. Tobin's book offers a humane alternative to the 'letting them cry' method. Her light-hearted approach and easy to follow recommendations will foster confidence and competence for any new (and exhausted!) parent. The Lull-A-Baby Sleep Plan gives parents the greatest gift of early childhood—SLEEP!"

—*Debra Phillips Hauser, PhD, lecturer, Child Study Center,*
Yale University School of Medicine

"Welcome to the Land of Nod: Dr. Tobin teaches us how to recognize and read our kids' cues so we can help them—and us!—get a better night's sleep. Her down-to-earth approach is refreshing. Great read for parents, new and old."

—*Kathryn Dorrell, Life editor,* Canadian Living *magazine*

"Perfect for bleary-eyed, exhausted parents who are in desperate need of solutions on how they can help their infant (and themselves) get some sleep. Keep this insightful reference handy; you'll refer to it again and again."

—*Sam Horn, author of* Tongue Fu! *and* What's Holding You Back?

"Dr. Tobin offers desperate parents an alternative to allowing their babies to control their lives or having to feel intense guilt by letting their babies 'cry it out' to force them to sleep. The Lull-A-Baby plan provides simple, gentle explanations and choices to help mom, dad, and baby sleep better. This book is an excellent resource for me, and one I will recommend to many new (and maybe not-so-new) parents!"

—*Kathee Andrews, MD, pediatrician, Toronto, Canada*

"The Lull-a-Baby Sleep Plan is the very best way to help *really* young babies sleep through the night!"

—*Denise MacNeil, RN, mother of three*

"I thought the first night would be the worst! I was so excited when my 3-month-old daughter, Paige, fell asleep on her own that I called Dr. C's office and left her this message: 'You were right about Paige being able to fall asleep on her own. But you were wrong when you said it would take about 20 minutes—it only took 10!'"

—*Camille*

"I'm pretty born-again about the Lull-a-Baby Sleep Plan. I followed the 7-day plan and even though I was exhausted, I didn't give up. It wasn't easy for me to listen to my baby fuss, but I never felt like I was deserting her. Thankfully, Cali began to sleep for longer stretches before the week was up."

—*Stephanie*

"This really works! Dr. C.'s advice completely changed my life and I have passed it on to others who now feel the same way!"

—*Lisa*

© 2006 by Cathryn Tobin, MD

All rights reserved. No part of this publication may be reproduced or transmitted in
any form or by any means, electronic or mechanical, including photocopying,
recording, or any other information storage and retrieval system, without the written
permission of the publisher.

Printed in the United States of America
Rodale Inc. makes every effort to use acid-free ♾, recycled paper ♻.

Illustrations by Jennifer Kalis
Book design by Anthony Serge

Library of Congress Cataloging-in-Publication Data

Tobin, Cathryn.
    The lull-a-baby sleep plan : the soothing, superfast way to help your new baby
sleep through the night ... and prevent sleep problems before they develop / Cathryn
Tobin.
        p.   cm.
    Includes bibliographical references
    ISBN-13 978-1-59486-222-9   paperback
    ISBN-10 1-59486-222-2   paperback
    1. Infants—Sleep—Popular works.   2. Sleep disorders in children—Prevention—
Popular works.   I. Title.
RJ506.S55T63 2006
618.92´8498—dc22   2006016282

Distributed to the trade by Holtzbrinck Publishers

2   4   6   8   10   9   7   5   3   1   paperback

We inspire and enable people to improve their lives and the world around them
For more of our products visit **rodalestore.com** or call 800-848-4735

To all the sweet little babies who love their parents so much, they just can't bear to say good night—this book is for you!

I am very excited to share my sleep secrets with you and your family! I hope not only to show your mom and dad how to gently guide you to the Land of Nod but also to explain to them what you need to enjoy uninterrupted sleep. My dream is to teach your parents, grandparents, health care professionals, and all baby lovers about the precious and fleeting opportunity that exists to create blissful and loving bedtimes. Don't worry—I'm sure your smart parents will master these new techniques in no time.

CONTENTS

PART ONE
LOOK WHO'S *NOT* SLEEPING!

CHAPTER ONE

CHAPTER TWO

CHAPTER THREE

CHAPTER FOUR

PART TWO
LOOK WHO'S SLEEPING
THROUGH THE NIGHT!

CHAPTER FIVE

CHAPTER SIX

CHAPTER SEVEN

CHAPTER EIGHT

CHAPTER NINE

CHAPTER TEN

Chapter Eleven

$\mathscr{A}$CKNOWLEDGMENTS

All truths are easy to understand once they are discovered;
the point is to discover them.

—Galileo Galilei

I have many people to thank for helping me see the truly amazing inner world of babies, and there are others to whom I owe my profound gratitude for their support, encouragement, and humor during this extraordinary journey.

- I am deeply grateful to all the trusting families who've chosen me to be their doctor and allowed me to be a part of their lives.
- It's impossible to capture the adoration I feel for the precious babies and children under my care who've allowed me to learn and grow along with them.
- Thanks to my late mother, Roselyn, a courageous woman who guided me to "never say never"; to my dear late father Sidney, whose unshakable determination and kindness will never be forgotten; and to my mother-in-law, Dr. Halina Solow, for her enormous enthusiasm and strength.

- My heartfelt appreciation to my editors, Heather Jackson and Mariska van Aalst, who helped me with great honesty, endless patience, and savvy advice during this long bookmaking process; to the superb organizing and writing talents of Debra Gordon; to Jennifer Kalis for her wit; and to my agents, Jackie Joiner and Denise Bukowski, for their capable and plentiful help and support.
- I am truly grateful to Connie, my receptionist extraordinaire, who is always willing to help—no matter what.
- And finally, the biggest thanks go to my husband, Henry, the kindest and most generous person I know in the whole wide world and my very best friend, and to my amazing and talented children, Benjamin, Marissa, Max, and Madison, who tolerated my endless hours at the laptop without complaint. Thank you all!

$\mathcal{N}$O MORE CRIB WARS!

Dear Mom and Dad,

What if I were to tell you that I've uncovered a secret that enables very young babies to sleep through the night—and that with the information I'm about to divulge in this book, you can begin to reap the benefits tonight?

When I hung up my shingle more than a decade ago, I had no idea how easily a very young infant could learn to sleep through the night. Like other baby doctors at the time, I assumed new parents simply had to accept and suffer from sleep deprivation. I totally empathized with dog-tired parents, but all I had to offer were flimsy platitudes like "This, too, shall pass" and "Try to nap during the day."

Even though research findings from the past 2 decades have provided us with a deeper understanding of the nature of infant sleep problems—including ineffective associations, inappropriate timing, and addictive nurse-to-sleep habits—these insights have not helped Mom and Dad get more sleep.

After completing my residency at the Hospital for Sick Children in Toronto, Canada, one of the world's busiest pediatric medical centers, it struck me that our culture goes about infant sleep training completely backward. *First* we allow bad sleep habits to form, *then* we go to extremes trying to break them!

Once I recognized this crucial mistake, the solution to the dreadful problem of sleep deprivation became crystal clear: Encourage young babies to develop good habits right from the start, and you won't need to break bad ones down the road. This insight led to the biggest breakthrough in infant sleep learning in years: the discovery of the *Window of Opportunity* (WOO) that exists to gently encourage terrific sleep habits.

The WOO is a precious and fleeting moment that begins around 6 weeks to 2 months of age, when a baby is ready to absorb good sleep habits—*provided she's exposed to them.* Unfortunately, the vast majority of parents and doctors don't know about this crucial time in their baby's development and fail to take advantage of this precious opportunity.

That's what *Lull-a-Baby* is all about. In the coming pages, I'll describe good sleep habits in infants, tell you how to identify when your infant is ready for the Lull-a-Baby training, and explain what to do if you've missed the magic WOO. Most important, I'll show you how to *lull* your tiny baby to sleep so neither he nor you feel any grief. You'll soon see that the true beauty of the Lull-a-Baby Sleep Plan is that a small baby needs only a tiny nudge to become a good sleeper.

Are you ready for more sleep? Then read on!

—Dr. C.

$\mathcal{I}$NTRODUCTION

WHAT IS THE LULL-A-BABY SLEEP PLAN?

Do you *really* need to send your baby off to boot camp or leave him to cry it out to encourage healthy sleep habits? Thankfully, the answer is no! After working as a pediatrician for more than a decade, carrying out more than 165,000 office consultations, and interviewing hundreds of families who have successfully used my Lull-a-Baby Sleep Plan, I have proof that:

- Even very young babies can learn to sleep through the night *without crying.*
- New parents can get the crucial sleep they need (finally!).
- There's a right time to begin sleep training, just as there's a right time to begin toilet teaching.

The Lull-a-Baby Sleep Plan is simple. Do the "right" thing at the "right" time, and your brilliant baby will sleep through the night. How can this possibly be true? Because babies are more capable than you think. During the Window of Opportunity (WOO), a baby's brain is hard at work, soaking up everything that's going on around him—including good (or bad) sleep habits.

It all depends on what you expose him to. Here's what you'll learn.

Part One of the Lull-a-Baby Sleep Plan explains the exciting but fleeting opportunity that exists to gently instill healthy sleep habits when a newborn wakes up to the world around him. Once you appreciate the importance of the WOO, your true options become clear— act early, or expose your baby (and you) to needless grief down the road. You'll also learn why current sleep methods such as Ferberizing and no-cry sleep solutions aren't necessary; the only humane approach is to *prevent* sleep problems in the first place. In addition, you'll become aware of the very real social, developmental, emotional, and health-related risks of sleep deprivation.

Part Two teaches you how to recognize the WOO and provides

HELPFUL HINT

Exhausted parents aching for more sleep might want to skip Part One and dive right into Part Two. In a few weeks, when your baby is sleeping better, you can backtrack and read the crucial background material.

you with the tools you need to take advantage of it—the Lull-a-Baby Sleep Plan. It also offers options if you've missed the WOO so you can solve your older baby's sleep problems by capitalizing on the unique talents of this age group. Plus, you'll find answers from A to Z-z-z for every conceivable baby sleep problem based on the crib-load of trade secrets I've picked up in my work as a baby doctor and midwife.

$\mathscr{P}$ART ONE

Look Who's *Not* Sleeping!

The Most Common Bedtime Mistakes
and the Price Parents and Babies Pay for Them

CHAPTER ONE

THE DANGERS OF SLEEP DEPRIVATION

People who say they sleep like a baby usually don't have one.

—Leo J. Burke

I returned to work when Gina was 6 months old. I was working as a nurse in the NICU [neonatal intensive care unit] at a large teaching hospital. My shifts were 10 to 12 hours long. Before I went back to work, Gina was sleeping 12 hours straight. From day one, however, she started getting up two or three times a night. I felt so guilty about being away from Gina that I didn't have the heart to say no to her when she woke up in the middle of the night. I thought I could manage with no sleep because my body was used to working the night shift. But last night, I learned I was wrong. While filling up my car with gas, I fell asleep at the pump! After the gas station attendants managed my spill, I realized it was time I manage my life!

—*Valerie, 28, mother of Gina, now 9 months*

Like many parents, you probably think of sleep as a passive state. In reality, however, your (and your baby's) body and brain are hard at work when you're sleeping. This is the time when your body produces important hormones and recovers from the day's wear and tear, while your brain actively reviews and files away knowledge, experience, and information gained during the course of the day. Sleep restores depleted energy supplies, rebuilds muscle tissue, tunes up the immune system, and rejuvenates the mind. Some psychologists believe sleep allows us to process significant emotional experiences and solidifies learning.

The Stages of Sleep

Understanding the stages of sleep will help you better understand the Lull-a-Baby Sleep Plan, as well as certain sleep problems that may occur with your baby.

There are two distinctly different types of sleep: REM (rapid eye movement) and non-REM. We do our dreaming during REM sleep, while most of the body's restorative processes occur during non-REM sleep. Until the Window of Opportunity (WOO) is wide open, a new baby enters REM sleep immediately after falling asleep, followed by REM/non-REM cycles and several brief awakenings. During REM sleep, a baby may smile (no, it's not gas!), twitch, grimace, breathe irregularly—and wake easily. In non-REM sleep, a newborn lies quietly and breathes deeply and regularly. At times, she may appear to have a burst of fast sucking or experience sudden body jerks.

The WOO begins to crack open when a baby is 6 weeks old. By 3 months of age, the WOO is wide open. Once a baby is about 3 months old, sleep cycles start with non-REM sleep, which develops into four separate stages that reflect progressively deeper states of sleep, from drowsiness to sound asleep.

THE TIMELINE OF THE WOO

The Window of Opportunity (WOO) begins to open around 6 weeks of age. It's wide open by 3 months and begins to close when your baby is 6 months old. By 9 months of age, it's closed tight. Think of the WOO as a process that gradually unfolds, peaks, and then fades away.

STAGE 1: Baby becomes drowsy and awareness of his surroundings diminishes. Even though his eyes are closed, his brain continues to soak up everything going on around him. If you try to put your baby down while he's in a light sleep, chances are good he'll wake up crying.

STAGE 2: As your baby continues to drift off and enter a deeper sleep state, his body functions slow, although he's still semiawake. To an onlooker, stages 1 and 2 appear similar. A baby may move around, open his eyes briefly, suck, or cry in response to distractions. Sleep researchers recognize this stage by monitoring brain waves.

STAGES 3 AND 4: These are the deepest and most restorative sleep stages. Blood pressure drops, breathing slows, muscles relax, blood supply to muscles increases, tissue repair occurs, energy is restored, and hormones are released. Stage 3 is the beginning of deep sleep. You may get away with vacuuming the nursery, but a sudden noise like a doorbell may disturb your baby's sleep. In stage 4—the deepest, most delicious sleep—you can lift your baby out of the crib, change his diaper, top him off with a moment at the breast or bottle, and pop him back in bed without waking him.

As stage 4 non-REM sleep evolves into REM sleep, a brief

(continued on page 8)

GLOSSARY

Throughout *Lull-a-Baby*, I use numerous terms original to the Lull-a-Baby Sleep Plan. This cheat sheet will help you keep track of them.

Age range index:

Newborn: Zero to 6 weeks—generally. Until the Window of Opportunity (WOO) opens, a baby is considered a newborn.

Younger baby: 6 weeks to 9 months. The time period during which the WOO occurs.

Older baby: 9 months to 1 year. After the WOO slams shut, an older baby's newfound skills can also help him learn to fall asleep.

Lull-a-Baby Golden Rule: Your baby must fall asleep in bed.

Lull-a-Baby Sleep Plan: The new, soothing, superfast way to help your baby sleep through the night.

> **Step 1: Identify and take advantage of the WOO.** When the timing's right, instituting healthy sleep habits is a gentle and agreeable process.
>
> **Step 2: Create "feel good" bedtimes.** Surround your baby with familiar sensations to trigger the sleep response.
>
> **Step 3: Charm your baby into sleepy contentment.** Use your voice, touch, and presence to soothe and lull your baby to sleep.

Self-start sleep: When a baby is put to bed sleepy but semi-awake and calmly nods off.

Stop, Look, and Listen: The steps you must take to really notice your baby and what her crying means.

- **Stop** yourself from racing to the crib every time you hear a peep.

- **Look** at your baby's face and body language.

- **Listen** to the tone, pitch, and rhythm of your baby's cry.

White noise, Oral ease, Wrap (WOW): The steps necessary to create the womblike feeling that helps your baby relax, let go, and fall asleep.

Window of Opportunity (WOO): The time frame when a baby naturally embraces good sleep habits if exposed to them.

Talk, Look, Cuddle (TLC): Steps that enable your baby to "zone out" the chaos around her. The calmer your baby feels, the easier she'll be able to guide herself to sleep.

- **Talk** to your baby in a perky tone.

- **Look** directly in your baby's eyes.

- **Cuddle** your baby's head in the palm of your hand at a 45-degree angle so you're looking straight into his eyes while you support his body on your forearm. This helps your baby feel less vulnerable and more connected with you.

Hang back, Empathize, Love, Persevere (H.E.L.P.): As one window closes, another one opens. Once your baby is 9 months, the window of opportunity to sleep-train a very young baby has passed, but the unique talents of older babies hold new promise.

arousal occurs, often at exactly the same time each night. Your baby may grunt, move about, and open his eyes to check his whereabouts. *These partial awakenings are a normal part of sleep*, but they present a major problem when a baby lacks the tools needed to doze off again. Many parents assume their baby is waking up because of hunger, when, in fact, the arousal is simply part of the sleep cycle.

REM SLEEP: About 90 minutes after falling asleep, a baby 3 months or older enters REM sleep, a state that reoccurs about every 90 minutes and lasts from 5 to 20 minutes. REM sleep is an active state, easily recognized as your baby's eyes move under his eyelids, and he twitches and maybe even smiles.

During this stage of sleep, bloodflow to the brain increases, dreams occur, your baby's eyes dart back and forth, and everyday noises usually won't rouse him. Your baby will have poor muscle tone; if he's in your arms, you'll notice his head and neck are floppy. Researchers believe that information and experiences are filed away during REM sleep, which ends with a brief arousal.

After the WOO opens, a typical sleep cycle looks something like this.

- Awake
- Drowsy (non-REM stage 1)
- Light sleep (non-REM stage 2)
- Deep sleep (non-REM stage 3)
- Deeper sleep for about an hour (non-REM stage 4)
- Light sleep (non-REM stage 2)
- Brief awakening
- Light sleep (non-REM stage 2)
- Deep sleep for 1 to 2 hours (non-REM stage 4)
- Light sleep (non-REM stage 2)
- REM sleep

- Brief awakening
- Light sleep (non-REM stage 2)
- REM sleep
- Brief awakening
- Light sleep (non-REM stage 2)
- REM sleep
- Brief awakening
- Light sleep (non-REM stage 2)
- Deep sleep (non-REM stage 3/4)
- Brief awakening
- REM sleep
- Brief awakening
- Light sleep (non-REM stage 2)
- Awake

Although the sleep stages are fascinating, the take-home message is this: Babies naturally and repeatedly wake up for brief periods throughout the night. A "good" sleeper settles down by herself and goes back to sleep with no help from you.

Is My Baby Getting Enough Sleep?

Although every baby is different, an infant's total sleep requirements during a 24-hour period are generally the same.

ZERO TO 4 WEEKS
HOURS OF SLEEP NEEDED: 16 TO 17

It doesn't matter whether you are breastfeeding or bottle-feeding; 4 to 5 hours (if you're lucky) is the longest you can expect a tiny baby to sleep at a stretch. Most newborns generally sleep just 1 to 3 hours at a spell. Because they don't have an internal clock that differentiates between

WHAT'S NEW IN SLEEP RESEARCH?

From the major research journals comes the following:

- Cuddling a baby against the skin for about an hour shortly after birth may help her sleep more soundly and for a longer stretch that first night in the world.

- Using a pacifier when a baby first goes to sleep may significantly reduce the risk of sudden infant death syndrome (SIDS). This is good news, but it presents a new and significant challenge for parents: How can an infant cultivate self-soothing skills if using a pacifier at bedtime? See page 41 for the answer.

- Swaddling a baby increases the amount of time spent in non-REM sleep and decreases the number of brief awakenings. For more on swaddling, see page 87.

- Television viewing among infants and toddlers is linked to irregular sleep schedules.

day and night, they sleep when they're tired. Thus, sleep comes in little sprinkles spread evenly over a 24-hour period. Newborn sleep begins with REM and may include several REM/non-REM cycles.

1 THROUGH 2 MONTHS
HOURS OF SLEEP NEEDED: 15½ (8½ AT NIGHT; 7 OF NAPS)

As the WOO begins to open, your baby spends more time awake during the day and sleeps for longer stretches at night. This happens, in part, because he's more alert, curious, and social and less overwhelmed by the world around him. Also, your baby's stomach is growing; now that it can hold more, he can go for longer stretches between feedings. Sleep stages also become more organized and more closely resemble those of adults.

3 THROUGH 6 MONTHS
HOURS OF SLEEP NEEDED: 15 (10 AT NIGHT, 5 OF NAPS)
At the beginning of this phase, the WOO is wide open but starts to close around 6 months. During this time, your baby forms sleep habits that will influence whether she wakes up and cries out for you or nods off again during natural arousals. Most babies have two daytime naps and a long stretch of sleep at night between 3 and 6 months of age.

7 THROUGH 11 MONTHS
HOURS OF SLEEP NEEDED: 15 (10 AT NIGHT, 5 OF NAPS)
During this time, your baby is still forming his sleep habits, although the distribution of sleep changes somewhat. After

(continued on page 14)

DID YOU KNOW?

We spend about one-third of our lives asleep. Here's the daily average requirement, by age.

Infants: 14–15 hours

1-year-olds: 14 hours

$1\frac{1}{2}$-year-olds: $13\frac{1}{2}$ hours

2-year-olds: 13 hours

Preschoolers (3–6 years): 11–13 hours

School-age children: 10–11 hours

Teenagers: $8\frac{1}{2}$–9 hours

HOW TIRED IS YOUR BABY?

Take this quiz to help you evaluate whether your baby's sleep needs are being met. Each point is not in itself a cause for concern, but when all are added together, the final score may suggest a problem with sleep deprivation.

Answer each question yes or no. Does your baby:

1. Conk out in the car before you pull out of the driveway? Y/N

2. Resist trying new foods? Y/N

3. Seem clumsy? Y/N

4. Fit the description "high maintenance"? Y/N

5. Need to be held all the time? Y/N

6. Act moody, high-strung, or touchy? Y/N

7. Grow increasingly hyper as the day goes by? Y/N

8. Wake up in a bad mood? Y/N

9. Reach milestones later than expected? Y/N

10. Constantly rub her eyes or struggle to support her head? Y/N

11. Fall asleep immediately when put in a stroller or swinging chair? Y/N

12. Yawn frequently? Y/N

13. Often fall asleep in your arms? Y/N

14. Seem highly impatient? Y/N

15. Demand inflexibility regarding routines? Y/N

16. Act slaphappy for a good chunk of the day? Y/N

17. Struggle with you at bedtime? Y/N

18. Handle frustration poorly? Y/N

19. Get less than the recommended age-appropriate amount of sleep? (see pages 10–14) Y/N

20. Fight naps? Y/N

TO SCORE: Count the number of "yes" answers. This is your total score. Here's how to interpret your results:

0–5: Your baby is not suffering from sleep deprivation.

6–10: Your baby has a challenging temperament.

11–15: Your baby needs more sleep.

16–20: Sleep deprivation is likely a problem.

6 months, babies should sleep for 9 to 12 uninterrupted hours at night and take one to three daytime naps of 30 minutes to 2 hours each.

12 MONTHS
HOURS OF SLEEP NEEDED: 14 (11 AT NIGHT, 3 OF NAPS)

By now the WOO has shut tight. Remember, however, that as one window closes, another opens. Your older baby has new talents and skills that enable you to help her overcome ineffective sleep habits.

Unfortunately, you can't just plop your baby on a scale to measure whether she's getting enough sleep. Instead, you have to learn to read her body language and monitor her behavior for signs of fatigue. One of my mothers told me she nicknamed her baby Cranky Frankie because he was so demanding. But once she learned to help him sleep through the night, the nickname no longer fit.

The Dangers of Sleep Deprivation

Sleep deprivation for infants is not benign. In fact, one study published in the journal *Early Human Development* found that 10-month-old babies with frequent night awakenings had lower mental-development scores than those who slept better.

Tragically, sleep deprivation is grossly underestimated and misdiagnosed in both parents and babies. Knowing the potential risks of sleep deprivation, however, will help you recognize that sleep is a necessity, not a luxury, for both you and your baby. Here's what you need to know about the effects of sleep deprivation on both your baby and yourself.

1. SLEEP DEPRIVATION MAY INTERFERE WITH YOUR BABY'S GROWTH. When we sleep, our bodies release growth

hormone, which helps build new bone and muscle, enables tissues to grow properly, and forms red blood cells that deliver oxygen to the brain. As you can imagine, this is particularly important for infants. Studies suggest that chronic sleep deprivation can alter levels of growth hormone in the blood, although it's not known if this impairs an infant's growth.

2. SLEEP DEPRIVATION MAY INCREASE YOUR BABY'S RISK OF SIDS. An article published in the journal *Pediatrics* found a possible link between sleep deprivation and a baby's risk of sudden infant death syndrome (SIDS). Researchers studied the sleep characteristics of babies who were kept awake at least 2 hours past their bedtime or naptime. They found that

HOW MUCH SLEEP
DOES YOUR CAT NEED?

About 16 hours. But there's a wide range of sleep needs among animals, as this list of average daily hours shows.

Lion: 20	Dog: 13
Chimpanzee: 12	Hamster: 13.5
Pig: 8	Gerbil: 13.1
Mouse: 12	Guinea pig: 9.4
Elephant: 4–6	Guppy: 7
Python: 18	

short-term sleep deprivation resulted in episodes of disrupted breathing combined with decreased ability to be aroused. It remains to be determined, however, whether these findings explain the increased incidence of SIDS that has been reported for sleep-deprived infants.

3. SLEEP DEPRIVATION MAKES YOU MORE ACCIDENT-PRONE. The National Highway Traffic Safety Administration estimates that sleep deprivation is responsible for more than 100,000 car accidents annually; in the National Sleep Foundation's 2004 Sleep in America Poll, 37 percent of drivers admitted to falling asleep at the wheel. One British study found that impaired driving was common among sleep-deprived mothers, who drove worse than drunk drivers. Being overtired impairs reaction times, increases aggressiveness, and interferes with judgment. Signs that you shouldn't be behind the wheel include frequent blinking or difficulty focusing, daydreaming, yawning, drifting into another lane, trouble keeping your head up, and irritability.

4. SLEEPY BABIES (AND PARENTS) GET SICK MORE OFTEN. If it seems you're constantly at the pediatrician's office, you may want to reflect on your baby's sleep habits. Sleep deprivation interferes with the body's natural ability to fight illness by making the immune system up to 30 percent less efficient. One study at the University of Chicago found that even modestly sleep-deprived kids were more vulnerable to infections. A key study by the same researchers revealed that a small sleep debt impairs the body's ability to process carbohydrates, manage stress, and maintain a proper balance of hormones—even among young, healthy people. Lack of sleep also accelerates

the aging process and increases risks of high blood pressure, heart disease, stroke, and memory loss. Several studies, including preliminary research at Brown University, link sleep deprivation with higher levels of cortisol. Chronically elevated levels of this stress hormone are associated with higher blood pressure, diabetes, and reduced immune responses.

5. FATIGUE ADDS UNWANTED POUNDS. Sleep deprivation whets the appetite by boosting levels of hormones that stimulate the growth of fat cells and raise blood sugar. Plus, it may lead to lower levels of leptin, a hormone that tells the body it's full. Chronic sleep deprivation also affects the way your body processes and stores carbohydrates, leading to weight gain. (Meanwhile, of course, you're more likely to choose a nap over a run.) Studies also suggest that poor sleep habits may contribute to the epidemic of childhood obesity. A study at Stanford University tied less sleep during childhood to later obesity, while researchers in Japan found a direct link between depth of sleep deprivation and degree of obesity: The fewer hours a child slept, the more he or she weighed.

6. SLEEP LOSS IS LINKED TO THE BLUES. According to researchers in Toronto, mothers suffering from postpartum depression are more likely to report that their babies wake at least three times a night.

7. TIRED BABIES ARE CRABBY—AND SO ARE THEIR PARENTS. Sleep-deprived babies are less willing to play on their own, and they get overstimulated more easily,

SIGNS OF SLEEP DEPRIVATION IN ADULTS

- You need an alarm clock to wake you.

- You depend on coffee to keep you alert.

- You long for a nap soon after you get up.

- You feel sleepy or doze off while watching TV, reading, driving, or engaging in other daily activities.

- Your nerves are shot.

- You become forgetful or clumsy, or your thinking is fuzzy.

- Exercise takes too much effort.

- You yawn all the time.

- You have difficulty keeping your mind on task, especially if the activity is boring.

- You feel pessimistic.

- You have road rage.

- You're easily stressed.

- Your stamina is low.

have trouble concentrating, cry more readily, and fuss at the breast or bottle. A chronically overtired baby may also appear giddy, hyper, moody, antsy, cranky, clumsy, or irritable. In fact, many babies considered "difficult" are just sleep-deprived. Lack of sleep also plays havoc with even the most loving parents' patience, transforming them into impatient, angry, and explosive people. As one exhausted mother told me: "My 6-month-old isn't sleeping well, and it's draining me. But it's my 18-month-old who's actually paying the price. This morning he spilled his juice, and I yelled so loud that you would have thought the house was on fire."

8. IT'S HARD TO REMEMBER THINGS WHEN YOU'RE EXHAUSTED. Another overtired new mother told me, "I was deeply inspired after watching *Oprah*. Too bad I can't remember a word of what she said!" During sleep, your brain files away new information, processes the day's events, replaces brain chemicals that contribute to memory and learning, solves problems, and prepares for the coming day—all fundamental to helping you form memories. Miss your rejuvenating sleep, and you'll be lucky to remember your own name!

Top 10 Baby Sleep Myths

Do you recognize yourself in any of these statements? Here's the truth about the most common misconceptions.

MYTH #1: MY BABY WAKES UP BECAUSE OF GAS. The most common reason older babies wake up and stay up is that they lack the self-calming tools necessary to manage night awakenings.

MYTH #2: MY BABY WAKES UP BECAUSE HE'S HUNGRY. Like adults, babies eat for reasons other than hunger. A baby will nurse because it's the only way he knows how to get back to sleep.

MYTH #3: MY BABY IS A POOR SLEEPER. We inadvertently train our babies to be poor sleepers by not equipping them with the skills they need to fall asleep.

MYTH #4: RICE CEREAL BEFORE BEDTIME WILL HELP MY BABY SLEEP LONGER. Hunger is typically not the cause of sleep problems after 3 to 4 months of age.

MYTH #5: CRYING DAMAGES A BABY'S PSYCHE. I've known babies who were raised on attachment parenting principles and those allowed to cry it out. Can I tell them apart by their intellectual, psychological, or emotional states? Absolutely not!

MYTH #6: IT'S EASIER TO SLEEP-TRAIN AN OLDER BABY. The longer a habit is reinforced, the harder it is to break.

MYTH #7: TEETHING DISRUPTS SLEEP. This may be true at times, but teething is blamed for way too many sleep problems.

MYTH #8: POOR SLEEP HABITS IMPROVE EVENTUALLY. Without their parents' help, the vast majority of babies will sleep worse, not better, over time. Sleep problems don't magically disappear. Consider the 2004 Sleep in America Poll, which found that two-thirds of children from infancy to age 10 experience frequent sleep problems.

MYTH #9: BABIES WILL GET THE SLEEP THEY NEED. If only! Babies resist sleep like similarly charged magnets resist each other. Parents need to insure a baby gets enough sleep.

MYTH #10: THERE'S NO HARM IN GETTING UP WITH MY BABY AS LONG AS I'M WILLING TO DO IT. If you enable unhealthy sleep habits, you run the risk of your child developing long-standing sleep problems that will persist into the preschool years.

CHAPTER TWO

THE TOP THREE SLEEP THEORIES—
AND HOW THEY MAKE MATTERS WORSE

Until now, the sleep debate has consisted of three opposing schools of thought:

- The cry-it-out theory from Richard Ferber, MD: A baby must be left to cry for a certain amount of time to develop independent sleep habits.
- The family-bed philosophy: It's natural for babies to wake up two or three times a night, and it's a parent's duty to soothe that baby.
- The no-cry solution: Parents can gradually (very gradually!) wean their babies of bad sleep habits.

Each approach has its merits, but none is ideal and none consistently works. Now there's a better option: the Lull-a-Baby Sleep Plan. It's the only proactive approach that focuses on establishing good sleep habits rather than breaking bad ones.

Behind the Cry-It-Out Plan

In 1985, Dr. Ferber looked back upon 10 years of research and developed his famous "Ferberizing" theory, recommending that babies learn to sleep for longer stretches using a "cry-it-out" strategy. The idea was that without Mom or Dad soothing her to sleep, a baby would be compelled to comfort herself before she dozed off, as well as if and when she woke up. The idea went like this:

After a relaxing and loving bedtime routine, Baby would be put into the crib awake and permitted to cry for short periods of time before Mom or Dad entered the room and offered reassurance. The baby would be left to cry it out for incrementally longer stretches each night. For instance, on the first night, baby might endure 5 minutes of crying before Mom came into the room and offered comfort; on the second night, Mom might wait 10 minutes before intervening; the third night, 15 minutes; and so on.

In my experience, this method works well with even-tempered babies who tend to go with the flow. However, it can be a horrendous experience with older, more intense or volatile babies, who go off like dynamite when their world overwhelms them. And once they lose

control, they shriek until they conk out or their parents cave in. What right-minded parent is going to hold back while her baby screams out a lung? Not many—that's why Ferberizing often fails. Some babies may indeed need to shed some tears (see "The Exception to the Rule" on page 26). But, I don't believe it's cruel to let an easygoing baby cry for a few minutes before she dozes off (all the hugs, kisses, and cuddles she's been getting all day make a short-lived aggravation a mere inconvenience). Nonetheless, I still have to wonder, is it *really* necessary?

The answer is a resounding no. I believe there is a more proactive way to solve sleep problems: Prevent them in the first place when you recognize your baby's WOO.

The Family Bed and Beyond

On the extreme opposite of the Ferberizers are the sleep martyrs. From dusk till dawn, they gratify their babies' needs, feeding on

THE EXCEPTION TO THE RULE:
WHEN BABIES NEED TO CRY THE BLUES

Although it brings me great pain to admit it, there are certain situations, such as after the WOO is long gone or when babies are confused by inconsistent sleep-training experiences, when a touch of crying may be needed as a last resort. If you're like most parents, 5 or 10 minutes of screaming feels like an eternity. I suspect babies feel the same way, so I advocate keeping crying to a minimum by popping in and out of the room. With you nearby, your baby won't feel his tears are going unanswered, and each time you drop in, you can reinforce that "I love you, but it's bedtime."

demand around-the-clock and often converting the marital bed into the family bed. These are the parents who listen to their hearts, not their heads. They firmly believe that the cry-it-out approach is a form of neglect that causes irreparable emotional damage and accuse Ferberites of detached, heartless parenting.

> THE THING THAT IMPRESSES ME
> MOST ABOUT AMERICA IS THE WAY
> PARENTS OBEY THEIR CHILDREN.
> —KING EDWARD VIII

The martyrs' method can be summed up this way: "When your baby is ready, she'll sleep through the night. In the meantime, it's your job to 'parent' her day and night." This is a classic example of the tail wagging the dog—babies direct their parents instead of the other way around. If Baby wants to nurse all night, Mom and Dad grin and bear it. Family-bed supporters nurse their baby to sleep, keep the little guy right next to them in bed, and feed him whenever he fusses during the night. This is reasonable for a newborn—but do older babies really need to feed every 3 hours at night?

As far as sleep regimens go, babies of sleep martyrs get the royal treatment. However, like royalty, they lead sheltered lives and often fail to develop basic self-calming skills. For example, if you race to comfort your baby at the first peep to spare her any grief, you inadvertently rob her of the opportunity to master her emotions. In my experience, babies raised in this manner are at risk of developing long-term sleep problems. If you are considering this style of parenting, ask yourself—before you drop from exhaustion—"Are these sacrifices truly beneficial?"

The Middle-of-the-Road Approach

For parents who desperately need to sleep but can't handle either the cry-it-out or family-bed approach, there's the no-cry option. Babies are gently encouraged out of bad habits and nudged into good ones.

Using sleep logs and questionnaires, parents learn to recognize their baby's ineffective sleep habits. Mom and Dad then apply different approaches until they hit upon something that works. The basic idea here is that babies can be phased out of bad habits slowly but surely. For instance, a new baby is encouraged to fall asleep without help by sometimes letting him fall asleep on his own, and other times not, and parents are encouraged to, as often as possible, stop feeding a baby before he drifts off. If he fusses, they are to give back the breast and try again later.

Like many ideals, this concept looks great on paper but is problematic in practice—it takes too long to get results. Many parents complain that they don't see any improvement after 2 months and give up from sheer exhaustion. This approach is gentle to a fault; it's impractical for anyone who wants to see progress in a timely fashion. Lori and Bruce discovered this for themselves.

The only way Matthew would fall asleep was if we drove around town with a Jimi Hendrix CD blasting. But when winter rolled around, it was too awkward to wrap Matthew into a snowsuit every time he needed a nap. My husband and I decided it was time for him to learn to fall asleep in

BABY BOOT CAMP

Warning: a new sleep technique has popped up. *Twelve Hours Sleep by Twelve Weeks* is basically an over-the-top cry-it-out approach. At 8 to 12 weeks, babies are put on a strict schedule. They're awakened, fed, and put to bed according to the clock. The philosophy is that Baby should fit into Mom and Dad's schedule, not the other way around.

Babies are "allowed" to feed every 4 hours during the day. If your baby is hungry earlier, you distract him. Babies are weaned off night feedings by being offered less and less to eat. And if she wants more? She's "allowed" to cry for 5 minutes.

Whatever happened to tuning in to your baby's needs or treating babies as thinking, feeling individuals? I'm sure this depersonalized, rigid approach means parents (and babies) get more sleep—but are such extreme measures *really* necessary?

his crib. Since I was set against letting him cry it out, we decided to try the *No-Cry Sleep Solution*.

I wanted Matthew to learn to fall asleep without breast-feeding, so I tried the Gentle Removal Plan. I was instructed to pull my nipple out of Matthew's mouth when he slowed down his feeding. I did this over and over, night after night. But after 3 months of trying without seeing any improvement, I eventually gave up. I blame myself that it didn't work. I probably gave up too soon.

The worst part is, since we tried this approach, Matthew's sleep habits have completely deteriorated. While initially it was hard to get Matthew to fall asleep, once he dozed off, he'd stay asleep for 6 to 8 hours. Now when Matthew wakes up, he refuses to go back to sleep. It looks like we're back to where we started—Jimi Hendrix and car rides—except now we need to drive for hours to keep Matthew asleep.

So Which Option Is Best?

The current sleep solutions all share a fatal flaw: They strive to solve sleep problems rather than prevent them. Clearly, crying it out is too brutal, and no-cry sleep solutions are too slow; the only ideal way to deal with sleep problems is to avoid them in the first place. That's where the Lull-a-Baby Sleep Plan comes in.

I prefer the Lull-a-Baby program because it's gentle and charming: You teach your baby to sleep by lavishing him with love. Thus, the Lull-a-Baby Sleep Plan buys you longer stretches of uninterrupted sleep with the least amount of grief. And you learn that when your timing is right, your baby will sleep.

CHAPTER THREE

THE INNOCENT MISTAKES DEVOTED MOMS AND DADS MAKE

Mistakes are the portals of discovery.

—James Joyce

To prevent sleep problems or fix ones that already exist, you need a firm grasp of what works and what doesn't. You must take a hard look at the common but disastrous sleep mistakes many parents make. I am not talking from up high in my ivory tower; as a parent, I've known my share of sleepless nights—many of my own making. But I've learned from my mistakes, and now I want to help you benefit from my hard-earned lessons.

Parents' 10 Most Common Sleep Mistakes

It's likely that at least one of these sleep-related slipups will ring all too true with you.

1. Encouraging unhealthy associations, such as rocking or nursing baby to sleep
2. Setting up the wrong bedtime milieu
3. Confusing "I'm so-o-o unhappy!" with "I'm so-o-o hungry!"
4. Putting a baby into the crib *already* asleep
5. Setting bedtime too late
6. Falling prey to new-parent anxiety, which may override common sense
7. Misunderstanding sleep cycles
8. Encouraging pacifier dependency
9. Delaying the inevitable: sleep teaching
10. Feeling guilty about wanting more sleep for yourself

Sleep Mistake #1: Encouraging Unhealthy Associations

> When my second son, Charlie, was 6 months, I stopped nursing him to sleep in the hope that he'd stop waking up at night. But I didn't have a clue how to help him sleep, and I couldn't stand to hear him cry. So I started rocking him in my arms until he dozed off. Unfortunately, I learned in retrospect that this wasn't too smart! Now, instead of waking up and nursing Charlie to sleep, I wake up and rock him—which takes me twice as long.
> —*Clarice, 24; Charlie, 9 months*

Aside from missing the Window of Opportunity (WOO), the worst mistakes parents make involve the steps they take to encourage sleep. While newborns are top-notch at breathing, sucking, crying, peeing, and pooping, Mother Nature forgot to equip them with dozing-off skills. Consequently, Mom and Dad need to help their baby learn an effective way to fall asleep.

Just what does that mean? It's when a baby is put into his crib sleepy but semiawake, and he calmly nods off. I call this self-start sleep, and a baby who knows how to do it sleeps better, deeper, and longer.

Unfortunately, tired parents tend to take the path of least resistance and dance, sing, jiggle, or nurse their little bundle to sleep. This, in turn, teaches a baby to rely on them for falling asleep and discourages development of the self-sufficient skills required for dozing off.

The bottom line: If you rock your baby to sleep, she will need to be rocked *each and every* time she's ready to nod off—not just at bedtime but also every few hours during the brief nighttime awakenings.

One young mom recently moaned to me, "The only place my 6-month-old daughter, Rachel, will fall asleep is beside me in bed. Obviously, she can fall asleep without being fed, so why won't she nod off in her crib?"

The answer is simple: Human beings are creatures of habit. We become accustomed to a routine, and any deviation causes us grief. In Rachel's mind, falling asleep is linked with cuddling next to Mom. No cuddles, no sleep!

After 5 years of struggling with infertility, I had no intention of letting my baby cry—not even an iota. When Jacob squeaked, my husband and I raced to the cradle and scooped him up. For months, I nursed, cuddled, and rocked Jacob back to sleep, sometimes three or four times a night. Initially, I cherished these delicious moments. However, after about 9 months, I began to feel drained. I stopped cooking meals, visiting friends, or taking Jacob out for walks. Eventually, I resorted to letting Jacob cry it out because I didn't know what else to do. I still feel guilty just thinking about it.

—*Penny, 31; Jacob, 1 year*

Sleep Mistake #2: Setting Up the Wrong Bedtime Milieu

Without fail, 2-month-old Barkley wakes up the instant my husband and I sit down for dinner. I wondered whether Barkley was waking up because he could smell our food, so I tried an experiment. Last night I made sandwiches. Curiously enough, Barkley woke up just as we took our first bite. Then it hit me. It's not the smell that wakes Barkley up—it's the quiet calm that descends when we eat.

—*Taryn, 28; Barkley, 2 months*

Baby experts recommend that parents keep bedtime calm because it's assumed that low-key activities help babies relax. That's great advice when older babies have forgotten the hypnotic rhythms of the womb, but understimulation actually drives younger babies bonkers! Scientists published an article in the prestigious journal *Sleep* that verified what moms have long suspected: During the last 10 weeks of pregnancy, fetuses sleep. This means newborns are accustomed to sleeping all twisted up like a pretzel, surrounded by quadraphonic sound blasting 24-7. Can you imagine how distressed a newborn must feel tucked away in a quiet nursery?

Contrary to what you might think, young babies sleep more soundly in a noisy milieu. They find white noise highly conducive to sleep (this is discussed in great detail on page 82).

Sleep Mistake #3: Confusing "I'm So-o-o Unhappy!" with "I'm So-o-o Hungry!"

Most of us wrongly assume that if a baby wakes up, he must be hungry. However, even if an infant feeds voraciously after waking, it doesn't necessarily mean he was actually hungry. Once a baby grows accustomed to nursing or sucking to sleep, he tends to rely on this method whenever he awakens briefly . . . which is likely to occur like clockwork every few hours a night.

Many parents continue to nurse or bottle-feed their babies at night because they're not sure when night feedings are "outgrown." Their confusion is understandable: Read popular parenting books and you'll find several conflicting opinions, like those below.

> Between 6 to 8 weeks and 4 months, babies might be hungry and need to bottle-feed two to three times a night, but after 4 months only once or twice; after 9 months, not at all. —*Healthy Sleep Habits, Happy Child,* Marc Weissbluth, MD
>
> Once your baby is 3 months old, he or she no longer needs to be fed at bedtime and again several more times during the night. —*Solve Your Child's Sleep Problems,* Richard Ferber, MD
>
> If a baby weighs 10 pounds and he's consuming at least 25 to 30 ounces of food during his daytime feeds or getting between six and eight breast feedings (four or five during the day; two or three clustered at night), he doesn't need an additional night feeding for nourishment. —*Secrets of the Baby Whisperer,* Tracy Hogg with Melinda Blau

No wonder parents are confused!

At the risk of confusing you further, here's my own guideline to help you gauge whether hunger is causing your baby's night awakenings. After carrying out more than 165,000 office consultations, I've found that a healthy baby who weighs 12 pounds or more can generally go 9 hours at night without feeding, providing she's fed well during the day. This generally occurs around 12 weeks of age.

Having said that, I still believe every baby deserves to be treated like an individual. Mom and Dad should be guided by *their baby's* needs and not by the needs of babies in general. Although the WOO begins to open around 6 weeks of age, that's too early to skip night feeds. Young babies have tiny tummies and need to suckle frequently, day and night. But that doesn't mean it's too early to encourage healthy sleep habits. As the WOO begins to open, encourage your baby to fall asleep on his own. Once he perfects this skill, he'll naturally begin to sleep for longer stretches. That's because a baby who knows how to relax and fall asleep won't be unhappy with brief night awakening. Instead, he'll quietly soothe himself back to sleep and wake up only when he's hungry.

Sleep Mistake #4: Putting Baby into the Crib Already Asleep

At Sam's 4-month checkup, his mother told me he was feeding every 3 hours at night. Jennifer confided that she was exhausted to the point of becoming absentminded, and she was losing her temper with her older child way too often.

I asked Jennifer whether she was putting Sam into his bed awake. She wasn't. But she said, "He won't fall asleep unless I rock him and sing a little jingle." I suggested she put Sam to bed sleepy-awake and stay by the bedside while quietly chanting the jingle.

The next week I received a thank-you card. "Although I seem to be forgetting many things," it said, "I won't forget your great advice! Sam is sleeping 8 hours straight."

Putting an infant to bed *after* she's fallen asleep is one of the worst mistakes a parent can make. For one, it's disorienting for a baby to wake up in her crib when the last thing she remembers is being cuddled in your arms. When the next brief night awakening occurs, your astute baby will realize she's no longer in your arms and scream at the top of her lungs.

Also, when your arms are the cradle that rocks her to sleep, a baby doesn't develop the self-soothing skills she needs to drift off on her own. You need to put your baby to bed sleepy-awake and lull her into a sleepy contentment. In Chapters Six, Seven, and Eight, I'll share everything you need to know to Lull-a-Baby to sleep.

Sleep Mistake # 5: Setting Bedtime Too Late

> Stella is like the Energizer Bunny. She refuses to go to sleep, and she's typically up past midnight. When she finally crashes, we don't move her because we're afraid to wake her.
> —*Ayumi, 22; Stella, 5 months*

When would you rather buckle down to a demanding project—when you're pumped or when you're pooped? I think most of us would agree it's best to tackle a task when we are at our best. Same with babies; they cope with challenges better when they have some energy reserved, which means starting bedtime *before* they are wiped out. This may seem counterintuitive, but babies manage bedtime best when they're sleepy instead of exhausted. A tired baby self-soothes more easily than one who's ready to crash.

Thus, it's important to recognize the "right" time to put your infant to bed. A baby can't say "I'm ready for bed" with words but communicates this message clearly through body language. Specifically, a tired baby:

- Rubs eyes
- Yawns
- Chews and sucks on own fingers
- Is happy but impatient; may be willing to play on the floor but demands attention after a few minutes
- Fusses and doesn't want to be put down
- Has a short attention span

By contrast, an overtired baby is slaphappy and hyperactive, with deteriorating coordination. This baby can't stay cheerful for long and avoids eye contact, refuses to cooperate, and cries and pitches tantrums. An overtired younger baby may arch her back, become floppy, turn away from you, cry harder if you try to console her, and cry at a very high volume and pitch.

Sleep Mistake #6: Falling Prey to New-Parent Anxiety

> I've been a first parent twice. The first time was 27 years ago, when my eldest was born. The second time was 10 years ago, with the birth of my second child. Both times I made the same mistakes I later came to regret.
> —*Tula, 41, mother of two*

Being a new parent is one of the most terrifying, overwhelming, yet glorious experiences on earth. However, the tidal wave of emotion seems to wipe out some of our rational thought processes. Many parents look back at their judgment calls and marvel, "How could I have done such a thing?" As Meg, a mother of three, said, "The first time around, I didn't really know what I was doing. I was just so grateful when my baby slept so I could finally get a moment's rest. Little did I know I'd still be rocking Lilly to sleep when she was 2 years old."

Sleep mistakes are easy to make but hard to correct. For instance, I've known many loving parents who understood full well that sucking on a bottle during the night can lead to tooth decay, yet they allowed their babies to have bottles in bed. One parent under my care explained, "We gave our son Tony a bottle in bed out of pure desperation. Now, 2 years and several cavities later, I'm deeply sorry for this mistake."

The point is that new parents, especially exhausted ones, are often inclined to make decisions they later come to regret. I'm referring not to any one specific decision but to the vast array of decisions new parents face. Ideally, new parents should think twice about the sleep habits they encourage by asking themselves, "Do I really want to be doing this a week, a month, or a year from now?"

Sleep Mistake #7: Misunderstanding Sleep Cycles

I thought I'd done everything right. I put Jimmy to bed awake so he'd learn to comfort himself to sleep. I stopped using a pacifier when he was able to find his thumb, and I didn't run to the crib when he cried. So why is the little rascal still fussing every few hours at night? I don't need to go to him, but he tosses, turns, and whimpers every 2 hours like clockwork.
—Vicky, 27; Jimmy, 6 months

Imagine a scuba diver as he jumps into the water and slips below the surface. Later he resurfaces, tanks up, and returns to the depths. Over and over, this cycle repeats.

Just like a diver, your baby's sleep goes from shallow to deep, and this cycle repeats itself five or six times each night (as described in Chapter One). Each sleep cycle lasts about 90 minutes. Many babies wake up fully after a brief night awakening because they don't know how to soothe themselves back into a deep sleep. They cry out as if to say, "Yo, Daddy! Do something quick . . . I can't sleep!"

While night awakenings are a biological fact, how a baby manages them is learned. The lesson for baby who's fed or rocked upon awakening: "When I wake up, warm milk [or rocking] helps me fall back to sleep." He comes to associate feeding with drifting off again, and this association becomes a deep-seated memory.

In Chapter Seven you will learn how to encourage effective sleep associations using the Lull-a-Baby Sleep Plan. You'll help your baby doze off by lavishing her with love. Initially, your efforts will be focused on bedtime and naptime. You'll feed the little lady as often as needed during the night. But an amazing thing will happen as your baby becomes more skilled at guiding herself to sleep. Around 3 months of age, she'll begin to sleep for longer stretches—just like that!

Sleep Mistake #8: Encouraging Pacifier Dependency

During a recent visit, a first-time mother of a 4-month-old said to me, "I'm doing everything right, yet my baby still wakes up every 2 hours."

> I ALWAYS WONDERED WHY BABIES SPEND SO MUCH TIME SUCKING THEIR THUMBS. THEN I TASTED BABY FOOD.
> —ROBERT ORBEN, AMERICAN HUMORIST

"I bet Michael is asleep when you put him in his crib," I said.

"No," she said. "He falls asleep on his own, but he still wakes up every few hours."

"How does he fall asleep?" I asked.

"He tosses and turns and eventually drifts off," she answered.

"Does he go to sleep with a pacifier?" I asked.

"Yes, and I have to pop it back in whenever he loses it."

"Bingo!"

Pacifiers are a mixed blessing. On the one hand, they allow tension to melt away. But at the same time, babies become dependent on them. That wouldn't be a problem, except young babies lose their pacifiers like toddlers lose mittens—especially in the middle of the night. And guess who has to get up and find them?

When a prop such as a pacifier is used to help a baby fall asleep, it becomes an integral part of the dozing-off routine. This means it needs to be handy each and every time a baby wakes up. In the above vignette, the mom got up every few hours throughout the night to pop the pacifier back in her son's mouth. Without it, he couldn't fall back to sleep.

A logical piece of advice might be to discourage pacifiers altogether. But the Amercian Academy of Pediatrics has thrown a wrench into the night by recommending that pacifiers be offered at bedtime and naptime to reduce the incidence of SIDS. They advise against reinserting the pacifier should your baby spit it out or lose it.

Safety always comes first, and therefore parents should respect this bit of advice. But it's crucial the pacifier not be offered later in the night, so your baby has an opportunity to develop more independent falling-asleep tools. Read more on this topic on page 84.

When I hear from a new parent that her baby is sleeping 12 hours at a stretch and has accomplished this all on her own, I always ask about thumb sucking. Almost always, the baby is indeed doing so. Thumb sucking is the perfect sleep charm—it's handy; it relieves stress instantly; and the baby's thumb never gets lost, wears out, or needs to be replaced.

Sleep Mistake #9: Delaying the Inevitable

Tina is an amazing mother. She has a developmentally delayed 2-year-old daughter and a feisty 9-month-old son. Months ago, she said, "I know you're going to be angry with me, but I'm still nursing Greg to sleep. I plan to work on his sleep habits next month."

The next time Tina was in the office, I asked, "So, are you getting any sleep?"

"Don't ask!"

Parents delay sleep training for a variety of good reasons. Many parents aren't aware that a WOO exists, some hold off in the hope that time will improve the situation, and still others are just too darn tired. But I feel sad when parents miss the WOO because I know that the longer they wait to deal with sleep habits, the more problems they're likely to face.

In my experience, once a baby is pulling up to stand, sleep habits have become ingrained and are much harder to change. That doesn't mean you can never break them, but doing so will take more time and ingenuity (an issue we'll address in more detail in Chapter Eleven).

Obviously, to avoid this altogether, I'd highly recommend you take advantage of the WOO—not just because you'd like more sleep but because it's easier on your baby.

Sleep Mistake #10: Feeling Guilty about Wanting More Sleep

Five-month-old Michael hadn't slept longer than an hour and a half at a stretch since the day he was born. His mother, Sandy, raced to his crib as soon as he made a peep because she didn't want him to feel deserted. After 5 months of sleepless nights, she was desperate for a good night's rest. But every time she even thought of encouraging Michael to sleep better, she felt overwhelmed with guilt, so she did nothing.

One morning, while driving, Sandy veered into oncoming traffic. Miraculously, no one was hurt—but her nerves were shattered. Then and there, Sandy realized the sleep sacrifices she was making weren't in Michael's best interest after all—his and her health and safety should come first. Guess who was sleeping through the night within the week?

Most parents don't realize the role that sleep habits play in their own health. They feel so guilty about wanting more sleep that they make unnecessary sacrifices. Luckily, the trends are changing as modern parents put a higher value on their own health needs. As one Generation X mom in my practice explained, "I'm a person *and* a mom, which means I try to balance everyone's needs—and that includes my own. Being a mom doesn't mean being a martyr."

That's pure win-win: Not only do you help yourself by encouraging good sleep habits, but you also meet one of your baby's fundamental health needs. A good night's rest is crucial for your baby's (and the family's) health, safety, and development. When you make sleep a priority, you're better equipped to handle the inevitable ups and downs of sleep training—and more likely to succeed at it. There are plenty of things to feel guilty about in life, but encouraging healthy sleep habits should not be one of them.

Thankfully, the slippery slope that leads to sleep deprivation is completely avoidable. Now that you know the danger spots, you can steer clear of them. But the perils don't end here. Not only do you need to know how to avoid mistakes, you also need to know how to encourage good sleep habits. In the next part of this book, you will learn the Lull-a-Baby Sleep Plan and how to nurture healthy sleep habits in your baby—right from the start.

CHAPTER FOUR

HOW TO SURVIVE—AND THRIVE—
BEFORE THE WOO OPENS

I survived the pregnancy, sailed through the birth—and just when I thought the hard work was done, I realized the end was nowhere in sight.

—Aasia, 22

Although this book is all about getting your baby to sleep through the night, there's no escaping the fact that for the first 6 to 8 weeks—sometimes a little longer—sleep will likely be a fond memory. This is the time between bringing Baby home and the opening of the Window of Opportunity (WOO). It's a time when getting enough sleep to even take the edge off your fog of exhaustion seems about as likely as winning the lottery.

That's because although newborns sleep about 16 out of every 24 hours, that sleep comes in tiny servings, which leaves you craving more. This is true whether your baby is breastfed or bottle-fed.

I love my baby like crazy and I shower her with attention,
but instead of feeling on top of the world, I feel like

47

I'm coming undone. I need sleep! How long can this
go on?
—*Paris, 35*

This lack of sleep is so endemic that some cultures have postpartum
rituals to relieve a new mother of normal household routines and
childcare responsibilities so she can simply rest. In our culture, of
course, with the exception of an occasional visit from the baby's
grandparents, sleep-deprived parents are generally forced to fend for
themselves.

I was tempted to go back to the office after the first week
because at least at work I'd get a coffee break.
—*Robin, 38*

Until the WOO appears, here's a primer to keep you afloat.

NEW BABIES HAVE NO CLUE ABOUT DAY AND NIGHT.
Instead, they sleep according to their internal biological clock
or circadian rhythm, which automatically sends signals of
hunger or sleepiness. Hence, they sleep about 2 to 4 hours; wake
for an hour of long feeding, play, and fussing; then sleep again.

YOUR BIOLOGICAL CLOCK IS NOTHING LIKE YOUR
BABY'S. Yours runs on a 24-hour schedule: You sleep at night
and are awake during the day. Thus, at least for now, you and
your newborn are on different wavelengths. Unfortunately,
you can't turn off your inner clock, so your brain will be
begging you to go to bed while your baby's erratic feeding
schedule forces you to stay up.

THIS, TOO, SHALL PASS. The good news is that your infant
will begin to differentiate between day and night between

6 and 9 weeks. Note the coincidence: Your baby's biological clock matures just as the WOO appears.

The Parent Power Nap

After Kelly, 27, mother of 6-month-old twins Katie and Kyle, discovered the dangers of extreme fatigue—she crashed through the garage door because she was so tired that she forgot to open it before backing up—she developed a newfound respect for naps.

Every adult has a specific sleep requirement. Genetics, in part, determines whether you need lots of sleep or can get by on a shoestring. If you don't get all you need, you build up a sleep debt. The only way to pay it back is to get extra sleep, over and above your everyday needs. Until you do, your body keeps sending out signals that it needs more sleep by making you feel more and more tired.

Because it's impossible for new parents to sleep for long stretches, the only way to repay the inevitable debt is to catnap. Naps are not for new parents alone, however. Researchers at NASA proved that 24-minute naps improve pilots' performances; Chris Carmichael, coach of cycling great Lance Armstrong, says naps were critical to Armstrong's overall training plan.

One of the biggest hurdles to napping is guilt: "I've got too much to do. I can't afford a nap." The truth is, you can't afford *not* to nap, so please ignore the voice in your head that says you're being lazy. A power nap is a brief, well-timed nap that gets you in and out of rejuvenating sleep as fast as possible.

Unlike real sleep, power naps include just the first two non-REM sleep stages: drowsiness and light sleep. You reap the restorative benefits of sleep—you feel more alert, energetic, and tolerant. Because you don't fall into a deep sleep, you don't wake up groggy. It's not enough to get you through every day, but it is enough to

POWER-NAPPING PEARLS

1. Give yourself permission to take a nap.

2. Keep yourself ready for naps. Don't try to remain awake with large amounts of coffee or other caffeinated drinks, which will make it harder to drop off.

3. Nap when your baby naps—but only in the morning and early afternoon. If you nap in the late afternoon, your body's biological clock is more likely to let you fall into a deep sleep, which leaves you feeling dazed. A 20-minute nap taken early in the day is more restorative than one of equal length taken later in the day.

4. Close the curtains and turn off the light, or wear eye shades. Darkness stimulates the sleep-inducing hormone melatonin.

5. Decide how long you're going to nap.

   - **Baby Boost: 2 to 5 minutes.** Curiously effective at renewing alertness.

   - **Mini Boost: 5 to 15 minutes.** Increases energy, motor performance, and ability to learn.

   - **Mommy Boost: 20 minutes.** Includes all of the above and improves long-term memory.

6. Set your alarm clock. Most likely your baby will still be sleeping when you wake up, but if you nap longer than 20 minutes or so, you'll be groggy. Now is the time to catch up on chores or enjoy some time for yourself.

help you get through *today*. It's like having a snack instead of an entire meal.

Keep Life Simple

The less stress you're under during this time, the better-quality sleep you'll get. Your mantra (for at least the first 6 weeks after birth—but hopefully longer) should be KISS: Keep It Simple, Sleepyhead. Here are some tips to help you pare down the pressures.

- ORGANIZE. When you design the baby's nursery and changing areas, think, "How can I create spaces that work?" Keep everything you need—diapers, wipes, creams, wastebasket, extra clothes—in strategic places around the house to minimize running around.

- GO FOR QUICK YET NUTRITIOUS MEALS. There are plenty of cookbooks dedicated to this goal. One of my favorites is Rachael Ray's *30-Minute Get Real Meals*.

- SKIP THE CLASSES. Do itsy-bitsy babies *really* need music-appreciation classes or alphabet flash cards? Absolutely not! Yet too many parents mistakenly think they'll deprive their babies of precious learning opportunities if they aren't enrolled in Gymboree, swimming, and baby yoga lessons before they're 6 months old. Skip the classes and savor the time with your baby.

- STOP THE MADNESS. Overscheduling children has become a raging phenomenon. If you need to color code the family calendar for your older children, you are doing too much.

- JUST SAY YES. Accept all offers of help. New babies need endless feeding, changing, and comforting, which doesn't leave much time for anything else unless someone can relieve you.

- KEEP "STUFF" TO A MINIMUM. Children don't need every new gadget on the market. There's less to clean up when your house isn't littered with toys, especially those that have dozens or hundreds of pieces.

- SCHEDULE TIME FOR YOURSELF. There will always be laundry to fold, dishes to wash, and floors to mop. Time for *you* won't exist unless you make it happen.

It Takes Two, Babe: Getting Him Involved

Jim felt he didn't need as much sleep as his wife. So for the first few months after Olivia's birth, whenever the baby cried, he jumped up, raced to the crib, and brought her to bed so his wife could feed her. When Olivia drifted back to sleep, he took her back to the nursery and popped her in bed.

Obviously, when you share night feedings like Jim and his wife, you also share the sleep debt. But this way, each of you "owes" less, so you're better able to maintain your sanity—plus, your relationship will be stronger if you share the work. Here are a few ways moms can help dads feel more involved.

- Before the baby is born, attend childbirth classes and (at least a few) prenatal appointments together.
- Don't hover when your partner is holding the baby or changing her diaper.
- Assume your partner is capable and let him do things his way.

- Anticipate that your partner will share in the care, but don't keep score.
- If you're breastfeeding, your partner can fetch the baby, change his diaper, and burp him after he's fed.
- Treat your partner as an equal, not an assistant.
- If your partner is taking the baby to the doctor, don't send along a note. He may not come back with an answer to every question you have, but he'll come back with his self-respect intact!

Partners, for your part, don't automatically hand over the baby to Mom whenever he fusses. You can discover ways to make Baby feel better by trying different calming techniques. You learn by doing.

Raise Baby's Comfort Level

At the first well-baby checkup, I told Dr. C. that Nina was terribly fussy. After examining Nina, Dr. C. reassured me my baby was healthy. "Then for goodness' sake, why does she wail like she's in pain?" I asked. "She's homesick," the doctor told me. Then she showed me how to swaddle Nina. It was like flipping a switch; all of a sudden, there was complete silence. In fact, Nina was so quiet that I had to check to make sure she was breathing.
—*Mary, 21; Nina, 3 months*

In addition to finding ways to stretch your endurance and get some sleep, it helps if you can find ways to make your baby more comfortable during this transition period, which may buy you some longer, less interrupted sleep. Here's what I recommend.

FIND REMINDERS FROM HOME. Often, when families travel with a young one, they bring along something like a teddy bear or blanket to help the child feel at home. But newborns come into the world empty-handed, so it's up to Mom and Dad to find some reminder of their baby's previous "home." One of the most effective ways to do this is to create a womblike atmosphere. That includes swaddling, offering a pacifier (a fetus begins sucking between 14 to 16 weeks gestation, which means she put in a lot of sucking mileage before birth), and creating white noise. Before the WOO appears, you can offer your baby a pacifier freely. But once she's tuned into the world around her, limit its use to bedtime and naptime. These steps will also be needed during the Lull-a-Baby Sleep Plan; you can read more on swaddling and white noise in Chapter Seven.

KEEP BABY CLOSE. Many parents keep their baby in a bassinet by the bedside, which makes for easier and quicker night feedings, without the potential dangers of cosleeping. For those who choose the family bed or resort to it out of exhaustion, read up on safety precautions on page 95.

MASSAGE YOUR BABY. Research suggests that touch has a powerful nurturing effect on babies; a noted pediatric journal reports that healthy preterm infants gained more weight after receiving a daily massage for 5 days than did similar babies who didn't get rubdowns. One of my favorite studies on the subject comes out of McGill University in Montreal, where researchers found that massage can actually raise a baby's IQ! Here's how to do it.

Choose a warm, comfortable place. Set up your massage area with a few soft towels, diapers, wipes, oil—cold-pressed vegetable, seed, or fruit, but not peanut or nut oil because of the risk of food allergies—and some background music all within easy reach.

Warm a small amount of oil between your palms. Begin at your baby's thighs, using long, firm strokes. This is the least intrusive way to begin because babies are used to their legs being touched during diaper changes. Move on to the feet, arms, hands, back, ears, face, chest, and tummy. However, don't apply pressure when you massage the tummy.

Never massage a baby when he's crying or upset. If your baby begins to fuss or become restless, it's time to end the massage. Babies are teeny, so it doesn't take long—10 minutes, tops.

Expect the 6-Week Peak

When baby Gail was 6 weeks, she began to have crying jags during which she'd turn red in the face, pull up her legs, and scream until she dropped from exhaustion. I assumed she had gas pain, so I watched my diet, administered antigas drops, and, when all else failed, booked an appointment with Dr. C.

Although Gail was weighed, measured, and thoroughly examined, I was skeptical (yet relieved) when Dr. C. said there was nothing wrong with her: "Have you heard of the 6-week peak?"

"No, what is it?"

"It's the moment before your baby steals your heart with a smile."

Just as she'd predicted, Gail's tears petered out over the next few weeks.

—*Ermie, 31; Gail, 2½ months*

Researchers have discovered that babies all over the world are fussiest and cry the most at 6 weeks. I suspect the reason is that as a baby becomes more intrigued by the world around her, she stops tuning it out. However, she doesn't know her limits and quickly becomes overwhelmed. Like a pot boiling over, she's pushed into frantic crying.

Luckily, this phase doesn't last too long. Soon she learns to turn down the heat, recognize her limits, and shut out the world when she's had enough. Not so coincidentally, the WOO begins to open as your baby perfects her off switch.

In the meantime, you have to survive this period. Anticipating and planning for it will help you get yourself and your baby through it.

The TLC Technique

When a baby is overwhelmed by the world around her but hasn't yet developed the resources to calm herself, you can help her focus on you and tune out the rest of the world by using TLC: Talk, Look, and Cuddle.

To be successful, you must do all of the following three steps together.

Talk to your baby. Use a perky tone of voice and chatter away.

Look directly into your baby's eyes—even if they're closed. Sooner or later, they'll open.

Cuddle your baby. Place your baby on his back, scoop your hand under his head, and pick him up by supporting his body on your forearm. Cuddle his head in the palm of your hand. Elevate his head about 45 degrees so you're looking straight into each other's eyes. Your baby will feel less vulnerable when elevated and will open his eyes and connect with you.

These steps will make TLC more effective.

- Swaddle your baby.
- Offer a pacifier or finger to suck on.

- Use movement. With your baby's head in your hand, move your arm up and down slowly, as though doing a biceps curl. This gentle back-and-forth motion will snap your baby out of a crying frenzy.

Use TLC whenever your baby is stuck in a crying jag. It will help her escape the frenzy she's experiencing and allow her nervous system to reset. It's like the pause between uterine contractions—one moment the tumult inside your body is overwhelming, and then suddenly the contraction fades, and you feel calm and composed. One happy father dubbed this new "trick" the Baby's Dimmer Switch. "It's the only way to guide my 1-month-old, Harris, out of his screaming fits."

Watch Out for Sleep Knots

In jest, I refer to the first few weeks of a baby's life as sleep knots because the routines established early on can leave us tied up in

> HABIT IS HABIT AND NOT TO BE FLUNG
> OUT OF THE WINDOW BY ANY MAN, BUT
> COAXED DOWNSTAIRS A STEP AT A TIME.
> —MARK TWAIN

knots. New babies (and often new parents) don't have a clue how to fall asleep or put themselves back to sleep during the night. As a result, many parents do whatever feels right at the time.

For example, first-time dad Brian couldn't get his 3-week-old son to sleep unless he nestled the baby against his chest. Unwittingly, he created a sleep knot that most likely will come back to haunt him; once a knot is tied, it won't loosen by itself.

The following are the most common sleep knots that develop during the newborn stage. If you don't untangle them before they tighten, be prepared to accept the consequences.

SLEEP KNOT #1: SLEEPING AT THE BOTTLE OR BREAST. A newborn gets used to falling asleep with something in her mouth, although by the time the WOO opens, she's perfectly capable of dozing off without it. She won't try to find other ways to fall asleep unless encouraged to do so.

SLEEP KNOT #2: THE PACIFIER. Initially, a pacifier calms a new baby and is as soothing as a toasty bath—until it's accidentally spit out. Then the little guy freaks out—he's lost the only way he knows to calm down. I recommend that when a baby is around 3 months old (which is when a baby can reliably get his thumb into his mouth), parents stop using a pacifier once he's drifted off so he has some motivation to discover his fingers or thumb, which are always readily available. (Don't remove the pacifier after Baby dozes off; just don't replace it after it falls out.)

SLEEP KNOT #3: ROCK-A-BYE BABY. For centuries, parents have jiggled, rocked, and bounced newborns to sleep. The rhythmic movement is so profoundly relaxing, it's almost hypnotic. But rocking becomes a sleep knot when a baby, especially an older one, can't fall asleep without it. This doesn't mean you should never rock a baby to sleep—that would be ludicrous. In fact, newborns often depend on rocking movements to help them relax and fall asleep. But it does mean that after your baby tunes in to the world around him, you need to modify your approach. As the WOO cracks open, the Lull-a-Baby Sleep Plan should kick in.

SLEEP KNOT #4: ASLEEP AT THE WHEEL. A car seat is like a nest, helping a baby feel safe and cozy. But it's a sleep knot when it's the only place baby will nod off and stay asleep. Luckily, swaddling creates the same sense of delicious comfort.

SLEEP KNOT #5: SLEEPING BEFORE BEDTIME. Allowing a baby to conk out in your arms may feel natural, but it quickly turns into a sleep knot when a baby can't fall asleep in her own bed.

You may have noticed that these habits are also integral ways to comfort a new baby. You should feel free to follow your instincts and soothe your new baby with these calming tricks. But as the WOO appears, these calming tricks suddenly "morph" into traps because they don't encourage mature babies to soothe themselves. So, as the WOO appears, trade these tricks for the Lull-a-Baby Sleep Plan. Your baby will appreciate the best of both worlds.

$\mathscr{P}$ART TWO

Look Who's Sleeping through the Night!

Finally! A Peaceful—And Superfast—
Way to Help New Babies Sleep Longer

A spoonful of sugar helps the medicine go down . . .

—Mary Poppins

ℭHAPTER FIVE

PREPARING FOR THE
LULL-A-BABY SLEEP PLAN

You wouldn't go out and run a marathon without first training, right? So why start sleep training your baby without getting into shape first?

Exhaustion is the number one reason for problems with the plan, which is why I want you to charge your batteries before you begin. Here's how.

BE COMMITTED. Before you begin to offer sleep encouragement, you need to be 100 percent committed to the approach. The strength of your conviction may go up and down like a yo-yo, but for your baby's sake, stick to the plan. If your conviction falters, please remind yourself about the serious risks of sleep deprivation by rereading the section beginning on page 14. Also, let me remind you, it's much harder (on your baby) to break ineffective sleep habits than it is to establish healthy ones right from the start.

UNDERSTAND SLEEP ITSELF. Being well informed about the nature of sleep (reread Chapters One and Three) will help you manage the "potholes" of sleep training without falling in. For example, you need to recognize that night awakenings are perfectly normal. The problem is when Baby can't fall back to sleep without Mom or Dad. Thus, your job is to help your child develop self-soothing back-to-sleep skills.

HAVE STAMINA. The sensation of being "mommy tired" (or "daddy tired") feels like you're running a marathon without a finish line. The antidote for this new level of exhaustion is naps—ideally, several tiny ones sprinkled throughout the day. Review Chapter Four for more on naps.

RETAIN YOUR SENSE OF HUMOR. The old saying that laughter is the best medicine is true. Laughing releases endorphins and reduces stress, leaving us feeling altogether better. Rent a funny movie, read a humorous book, visit a comedy club (without your baby). The more relaxed you feel during this journey, the easier it will be to tolerate the speed bumps.

REMAIN OPTIMISTIC. Who's more likely to succeed—a mother filled with doubts about the process or one with complete confidence in herself and her child?

GET SOME FRESH AIR. The brain is wired to sleep when it's dark and stay awake when it's light. Thus, staying indoors all day can knock your and your baby's biological clocks off-kilter. The two of you should get outside every day for a long walk, even in chilly weather. The fresh air will do both of you good and help you both sleep better.

KEEP LIFE SIMPLE. Keep activities to a bare minimum once you begin sleep training. Plan distractions for your other children so you don't feel pulled in opposite directions.

Know Your Baby's Temperament

Some babies are highly emotional: They can go from blissfully happy to utterly miserable in a millisecond. Luckily, they also leap from misery to total bliss just as quickly. Part of successfully using the Lull-a-Baby Sleep Plan involves knowing your baby's temperament. This allows you to predict the degree of sleep complications you're likely to encounter, be proactive, minimize problems, and maximize success.

About 40 percent of babies are considered "easy." These happy, flexible, easygoing individuals are open to new situations. Ten percent of babies are "spirited" or "difficult"; they're more energetic, sensitive, persistent, passionate, stubborn, and resistant to change than so-called easy babies. About 15 percent of infants fall in between—they're easy to upset but also easy to settle. The remaining 35 percent of babies defy labeling; they're easygoing in some situations and difficult in others.

The key, of course, is figuring out your baby's temperament. This is important because it will help you anticipate problems. For example, if your baby is skittish or volatile, it's unlikely that sucking on his lower lip or staring off into space will be enough to settle him down in the middle of the night. The knowledge that your baby is likely to need extra support allows you to plan ahead: Take more naps, devise a schedule with your partner, or line up family and friends to pitch in.

Answering the following questions will help you identify your baby's temperament, enabling you to predict problem areas and plan ahead for them during the Lull-a-Baby process.

1. Does your baby whimper or wail when you undress him?
2. When your baby is hungry, does she whine like a puppy or roar like a lion?
3. Does your baby "go with the flow" or startle easily?

4. If your baby is uncomfortable, does he gradually become fussy or begin screaming right away?

5. Is your baby easy to calm down once he gets himself worked up, or does it take a long time and huge effort to settle him down?

6. Does your baby enjoy playing by herself, or does she get bored easily?

If the second half of each question best describes your baby, he likely has a more intense or sensitive temperament.

Now that you know more about your baby's personality, it's time to begin the Lull-a-Baby Sleep Plan.

Learn the Lull-a-Baby Golden Rule

Here it is: Your baby must fall asleep in bed.

Notice I say "bed," not "crib"; that's because this technique will work equally well regardless of whether you're bed sharing, using a side bed, or putting your baby to sleep in a crib in his own room. It doesn't matter where he's put to bed, as long as he goes there sleepy-awake.

Very quickly, you'll find that you can woo your baby to sleep without taking her out of the crib. Here's how one mother interpreted the Golden Rule.

> Dr. C. said, "Do whatever you want, as long as your baby falls asleep in his bed." So I crawled into the crib with my son. I'm so tiny, I fit. I cuddled up next to my 3-month-old, Paul, and sang him a lullaby until he dozed off. I did this for three nights. On the fourth night, I sat beside the

crib and sang the same lullaby—and lo and behold, Paul
dozed off. The next night, I sang the usual lullaby before
placing him in his crib—and Paul fell asleep on his own.
—*Mabel, 19*

Now, I'm not suggesting you crawl into the crib with your baby. In
fact, I'd advise against it. However, lullabies are lovely, and I encourage
you to think as creatively as this mother did.

CHAPTER SIX

STEP ONE: WATCH OUT FOR THE WOO

God could not be everywhere so he made mothers.

—Jewish Proverb

The Lull-a-Baby Sleep Plan is about doing the "right" thing at the "right" time. Before we get down to the specifics, however, let's talk about the theory behind the method.

Three-year-olds can be potty trained; 9-month-olds can't. The same idea applies to sleep. Everyone assumes that encouraging babies to fall asleep on their own stresses them out. Those naysayers are wrong. When the timing's right, instituting healthy sleep habits is a gentle and even agreeable process. On the other hand, what really causes an infant grief is being forced to break old routines. *Sleep training is not hard; breaking bad habits is.*

One evening, as I walked by the newborn nursery in my community hospital, I noticed a nurse sitting quietly and working on charts while 23 babies slept peacefully in their bassinets. "What luck!" I thought. "All the babies asleep at once." The next night, a different nurse was on duty; the nursery was full; and to my great shock, the majority of babies were again sound asleep. It struck me that this was no coincidence.

So I tiptoed into the nursery and whispered, "What's your secret? How do you get all the babies to fall asleep at the same time?" The nurse smiled and said, "We just make them feel at home." Before she had a chance to explain, a newborn in the corner stirred, and the nurse left to comfort her.

Watching the nurses perform their magic became part of my daily rounds. After visiting my in-hospital patients, I'd stop by the nursery and watch the pros swaddle, feed, and comfort babies who had just come into this world. Most important, I noted how calm and confident these caregivers were in their ministrations. I didn't see any anxiety, angst, or apprehension—only composure and capability.

Newborns may not sleep for long stretches, but there's a lesson to be learned from how they fall asleep. When I blended the best of what I'd observed from the pediatric nurses with the wisdom I'd picked up during my midwifery stint and the scientific reasoning behind my medical training, I discovered something truly amazing: Babies come with a sleep "button"—and when you push it, you trigger a profound sense of relaxation, which I coined the *sleep response*.

To understand how pushing your baby's sleep button works, think about what happens when someone pushes your button. If, say, someone steals your parking spot or sneaks in front of you in line, physical changes occur. Your heart pounds, your face turns red, your voice rises, your palms sweat, and you feel a rush of energy. When you face a stressful situation, real or imagined, your body releases stress hormones as part of the fight-or-flight response—your state of arousal, heart and breathing rates, blood pressure, and muscle tension all increase.

Now imagine a different button, one with the opposite effect on your system. Push it and your heart rate decreases, your shoulders relax, your breathing slows, and you experience an overall sense of well-being.

The relaxation response was described by Harvard professor Herbert Benson, MD, in 1976. The first is the stress response; the second, the relaxation response. Just as stimulating one area of the brain elicits the stress response, activating other areas reduces it.

The *sleep response* occurs when you stimulate areas of the brain that control relaxation—that is, when you push your baby's sleep button. These techniques are not new; they've been practiced by knowledgeable parents, midwives, and baby nurses for centuries. What's new is the complementary manner in which they're used.

None of the components on its own can activate the sleep response. When used together and properly, however, they act synergistically and Lull-a-Baby to sleep.

Like a password, the steps must be entered correctly; otherwise, either nothing happens or your baby gets upset. Do it the right way, and he melts like butter.

Take Advantage of the WOO

When your baby is born, you count her fingers and toes and feel a tremendous sense of relief when you reach 10. But what is not as readily apparent is that when a human baby arrives in this world, she's not fully developed—her nervous system and brain are still works in progress.

At birth, a newborn baby's brain is one-quarter the weight of an adult's. Although it contains about a hundred billion cells, they need to be connected before they'll work. These connections are called synapses. By 3 months, the synapses will have multiplied more than 20 times, and the speed at which brain cells transmit information will have also increased as the developing brain lays down a fatty substance called myelin.

Once these brain changes occur, your baby is ready to take cues from the environment, learn, and file away memories. When your 2-month-old flashes a smile, she's telling you that her mental abilities have blossomed, her neural circuits have matured, and she is now capable of learning and remembering. As your brilliant baby becomes an active participant in your relationship, the WOO—the Window of Opportunity—to encourage healthy sleep habits begins to open.

During this critical period, specific experiences have greater impact. It's similar to what happens when newly hatched chicks follow *any* moving figure and quickly develop "mother figure" attachments. We know this as "imprinting," defined as a "rapid and irrevocable learning process occurring early in life." Likewise, when a newborn comes out of his cocoon and "wakes up" to the world around him, the first sleep habits he's exposed to are the ones that stick. You have now entered the WOO—the ideal time to nudge your baby toward healthy sleep habits.

The Window of Opportunity Timeline

Most of us have a basic grasp of infant development. We know sitting comes before crawling, which precedes walking. When we pay attention to more subtle accomplishments, however, we notice a baby's evolving awareness of the world around him and can best gauge his proximity to the WOO. Here's how the time-line works.

Zero to 3 weeks: *The WOO is closed tight.*

With a hundred billion brain cells not yet wired and a brain just 25 percent of adult size, a newborn:

- Can see only 12 inches
- Notices movement and contrast, but everything else is a blur
- Sometimes gets stuck staring at one thing
- Cries when upset (but not to communicate with you; just complaining to himself)

3 to 6 weeks: *The WOO remains shut.*

Although still not an active participant in the world around her, your baby becomes more aware of her surroundings, with well-developed senses of hearing and smell. A baby this age:

- Has yet to smile, make eye contact, control her arms or legs, or keep her head up
- Clenches hands into fists; holds head steady for just a few seconds
- Keeps eyes closed to prevent overwhelmed feeling
- Cries with greater intensity, from a whimper to a wail
- Startles easily
- Will grasp a finger
- Still spends most of the time feeding, sleeping, or crying

6 to 8 weeks: *The WOO begins to open.*

The part of the brain that manages emotion undergoes rapid growth. Vision is dramatically improved, and your baby can now discern color and detail and becomes interested in the external world. Your baby:

- Gazes up at you and smiles for first time
- Can briefly hold up head
- Recognizes and calms to parent's voice
- Is outgrowing sucking reflex and can now suck voluntarily
- Has stronger neck muscles
- Can track object with eyes
- Coos back at you

8 to 16 weeks: The WOO is wide open.

Different parts of your baby's brain mature at different speeds. Your baby can socialize and she's beginning to be able to control her emotions. A baby this age:

- Begins to babble
- Imitates facial expressions
- Shows interest in the external world
- Uses body language to show emotions, such as scrunching up face and pouting when upset
- Plays independently for 10 to 15 minutes
- Is getting close to turning over

16 to 28 weeks: The WOO begins to close.

By 4 months, your baby has developed binocular vision (can focus both eyes at once), which creates depth perception; by 6 months, she notices shadows, shading, perspective, and size. She can learn new habits—but must be weaned from old ones first. During this period, a baby:

- Reaches for objects
- Sits up, but may initially need support

• Has developed a falling-asleep routine and is not likely to give it up without a fight

9 months and older: The WOO slams shut (for now).

Your baby sees himself as a separate person, with his own personality and perspective. As the brain's memory center matures, attachment to parent(s) may strengthen, as does understanding of cause and effect, complicating bedtime. Your baby:

• Is well coordinated
• Babbles and uses tone of voice to express feelings
• Is more independent
• Cries when loved ones are out of sight
• Remembers routines
• Cries when put to bed because he knows Mom or Dad will now disappear

Like Goldilocks, who couldn't sleep until she found a bed that felt "just right," parents also need to recognize there's a "just right" time to start sleep training. I'm deeply disappointed when a family misses the WOO because I know how much harder sleep training will be. On page 78, you'll find my timeline, which will help you keep track of your baby's progress. When your baby meets three out of four milestones in the "Just Right" column, it's time to begin.

Beyond Excuses

Since the signs of the WOO are so obvious, why don't all parents take advantage of it to teach their children good sleep habits? Several reasons.

EXCUSE #1: I WAS TOO TIRED. By far the most common reason I hear is pure exhaustion. It takes more energy to coach your child to sleep than it does to comfort him until he dozes off.

EXCUSE #2: I WAS SCARED THE BABY WOULD WAKE THE NEIGHBORS OR THE REST OF THE FAMILY. Sometimes it's hard to allow your baby to fuss because you're worried about bothering others. When you Lull-a-Baby to sleep, however, the process is quiet.

EXCUSE #3: I DOUBT IT WILL WORK FOR MY BABY. Some babies are higher maintenance than others, but every baby is capable of sleeping for longer stretches when the right technique is used.

EXCUSE #4: MY PARTNER CAN'T STAND TO HEAR THE BABY CRY. Following the Lull-a-Baby plan may include some fussing, but crying is unnecessary.

EXCUSE #5: TIME FLIES. "I planned to work on my baby's sleep habits, but by the time I was ready to begin, I'd already missed the Window of Opportunity." In that case, you can still use the Lull-a-Baby Sleep Plan. (See Chapter Eleven.)

Common Questions about the WOO

I'm sure you'll find some of your questions in this list.

> IS THERE A DOWNSIDE TO BEGINNING SLEEP LEARNING EARLY? No. If you can steer your baby toward healthy sleep habits right from the start, you'll spare everyone grief in the long run.

	Too Early	**Getting Closer**	
SLEEP STYLE	Doesn't differentiate between day and night Sleeps about 16 out of every 24 hours	Still sleeps and wakes in a continuum without day-and-night differentiation but begins to sleep for longer stretches at night	
SOCIAL ABILITIES	Quiets when picked up Prefers high-pitched tones Shuts out unwanted stimuli Doesn't focus on your face	Smiles in sleep but not responsively Alert about 1 hour total in the day and night Likes being talked to	
SENSORY ABILITIES	Stops sucking to look at objects Focuses on objects 8 to 12 inches away Loves looking directly at light Responds to loud noises by grimacing	Is soothed by faces Facial expression does not reveal feelings	
MOTOR ABILITIES	Can't get fingers into mouth and keep them there Goes cross-eyed when looking at objects close-up Head flops if not supported No control over body movements Keeps hands fisted	Practices flexing arms Less floppy	

· WILL I BE EXPECTED TO LET MY BABY CRY IT OUT? Absolutely not! Young babies will likely fuss a bit. But never, ever would I suggest you leave a teeny baby to cry it out. It wouldn't be fair, and it isn't necessary.

· WHAT IF I MISS THE WINDOW OF OPPORTUNITY? Don't worry—lulling your baby to sleep still works; it just requires more time and ingenuity. (See Chapter Eleven.)

Almost There	Just Right	Too Late
Less daytime sleep, more night-time sleep	No more day/night confusion	Pulls self up in crib and calls out for you upon awakening
Makes brief eye contact	Recognizes parents from a distance Quiets to a soothing voice Enjoys playing with others Imitates social expressions Reaches for you	Shows affection for special people Stranger anxiety is present Distinguishes between people she knows and those less familiar
Calms when held Studies your face while feeding Prefers to look at high-contrast patterns and faces	Studies faces Makes eye contact Notices own hands Tracks moving objects	Coos and gurgles Facial expressions communicate mood Watches other faces intently Smiles at sound of your voice Turns head to direction of sound
May dig heels into mattress and inch self forward Can lift head slightly when lying on tummy	Head doesn't lag when baby is pulled to sitting Holds head at midline Can lift head to 45 degrees when lying on tummy	Grasps rattle when handed one Hands held open or lightly fisted Supports body with arms when lying on tummy Swipes at dangling objects Reaches for toys Can stretch limbs Plays with hands Supports head when still

· WHAT ARE THE MOST OBVIOUS SIGNS THAT IT'S TIME TO ENCOURAGE HEALTHY SLEEP HABITS? Purposeful smiles and coos clearly reflect that the WOO is wide open.

· WILL EARLY SLEEP TRAINING INTERFERE WITH BREASTFEEDING? Not an iota. The beauty of this method is that babies stop waking up—except when hunger calls.

Trust me! Many mothers and fathers decide, "I don't have the energy to deal with my baby's sleep habits right now." Some of these families will get lucky; their babies will turn their sleep habits around without a major fuss. But the vast majority of parents will look back with regret and promise, "I won't make the same mistake next time around."

CHAPTER SEVEN

STEP TWO: CREATE "FEEL GOOD" BEDTIMES

Babies are such a nice way to start people.

—Don Herold

Now that the time is right and the window of opportunity (WOO) is wide open, get ready to soothe your baby to sleep. Every component of the Lull-a-Baby Sleep Plan is designed to trigger a profound sense of contentment that allows your baby to relax, let go, and fall asleep. As we discussed, this is called the sleep response.

Just a reminder: You trigger the sleep response by surrounding a baby with the womblike conditions he associates with sleep from his days as a fetus. The most effective bedtime soothing techniques can be divided into the following three categories:

1. White noise
2. Oral ease
3. Wrap

The acronym for this popular soothing method is WOW! The idea came from the feedback I received after introducing this method to families under my care. Once they saw how well it worked, they said, "Wow! I'm finally getting some sleep," "Wow! Bedtime is a breeze," "Wow! Jake is sleeping better than ever," and "Wow, I can't believe Cindy is sleeping through the night! She's only 10 weeks old."

The following is a detailed description of each aspect of WOW. I highly recommend you begin this bedtime regimen right after your baby is born so you can perfect each component before it's needed. Besides, as we discussed in Chapter Four, newborn babies also love sensations that remind them of the womb.

W: White Noise

Researchers who inserted a hydrophone into a pregnant mother's uterus heard a cacophony of noises: blood whooshing, stomach gur-

> HE WHO SLEEPS IN CONTINUAL
> NOISE IS WAKENED BY SILENCE.
> —WILLIAM DEAN HOWELLS

gling, and Mom's colorful voice speaking. Thus, for 9 months, a fetus bathes in a symphony of sounds. It's like growing up with the ocean in your backyard: The sound of the waves serenades you day and night. The whooshing is so familiar that you no longer hear it—until one day you move away. Suddenly, the silence is deafening. You find it hard to concentrate and sleep. Without undulating waves, you feel lost.

After 9 months of sleeping in surround sound, a new baby suffers a similar silence shock, particularly at bedtime, when the whole house-

PARENTS' TOP SEVEN QUESTIONS ABOUT WHITE NOISE

1. **When should I begin to use white noise?** Once the WOO opens, it's time to develop an atmosphere that encourages sleep. However, many newborns sleep better with white noise, so I'd have to say begin at the beginning.

2. **How loud should white noise be?** Every baby is different. Some like it loud; others, soft. Start with a hint of white noise and gradually increase it until your baby quiets. Don't be surprised if you need to crank it up as loud as a rock concert. Also, try keeping the source of the noise close to the baby so he can feel vibrations from the source (but not close enough that he can reach it).

3. **Should I use white noise all night?** Initially, white noise should be used overnight. Once a baby gains the skills to fall asleep and stay asleep, you can stop.

4. **Will my baby become addicted to white noise?** No. Young babies' needs differ from those of older babies. Young babies are soothed by white noise, while older babies are indifferent to it.

5. **Will white noise cure my baby's sleep problem?** No. White noise allows a baby to gather her wits about her. Once she's calmed herself down, she can wiggle around and explore new ways to comfort herself.

6. **What if white noise doesn't work?** Occasionally, a young baby is indifferent to or irritated by white noise. Just turn it off.

7. **Are there any side effects?** None whatsoever.

hold tiptoes around for her benefit. Instead of making a huge effort to keep the house quiet "so the baby can sleep," give her a healthy dose of noise, which is what she really needs. New babies crave noise until 3 to 4 months of age. White noise is best because it soothes instead of stimulates, calming a young baby's simmering nerves. It inundates the ear with a multitude of tones to the point that the brain stops trying to distinguish one sound from another and surrenders to its relaxing nature.

You don't have to buy some fancy white-noise machine. Here are six items that you probably have around the house:

1. Radio tuned to static
2. Television station tuned to a scrambled cable channel
3. Fan
4. Vacuum
5. Treadmill
6. Vaporizer

O: Oral Ease

> I followed the Lull-a-Baby Sleep Plan except for one thing: I didn't take Laura's pacifier away when she dozed off. There was many a time I wish I had because Laura kept waking up each time she lost it.
> —*Kelly, age 36, mother of two*

By 5 months, studies find, a fetus sucks its thumb and the umbilical cord and even licks the uterine wall. Many babies are born with calluses on their fingers or thumbs from intensive sucking. However, after birth, babies can't suck their thumbs, fingers, or toes because their limbs won't obey. A baby may twist, turn, and root, looking for something to put in his mouth. Parents assume this means the baby is hungry, but often, he just wants to suck on something . . . anything! That's when a pacifier comes into the picture.

Pacifiers made their debut appearance in a painting of the Madonna and Child at the beginning of the 16th century. In the 1800s, well-to-do mothers gave babies pacifiers made of silver. Pacifiers were also available in coral and mother-of-pearl, while a less elaborate version, the "sugar teat," was made by wrapping sugar in a cloth and soaking it. In the early 1900s, Sears and Roebuck advertised a pacifier that resembles today's versions. Pacifiers have even become a fashion accessory for teens. They've been around so long because they make babies feel good. Studies have shown that sucking stimulates the release of chemicals in a baby's brain that decrease stress, heart rate, blood pressure, and pain.

Nonetheless, I believe the pacifier is both a godsend and a complete nuisance. Although it's a splendid calming tool, getting up at night to pop a "nummy" in your baby's mouth every time she loses it might be considered a tad inconvenient.

But safety takes precedence over convenience—recall the study mentioned earlier that suggests that pacifiers may reduce the risk of sudden infant death syndrome (SIDS)—so, early on, a pacifier should be used at naptime and bedtime. However, when your baby turns 3 months, instead of popping a pacifier back in your baby's mouth during the wee hours, let him enjoy his thumb. He'll sleep better, and so will you.

If your baby doesn't want a pacifier, don't force it. But here's a trick that may help change an infant's mind: The next time your baby is upset, wash your hands and offer your little finger to be sucked on. Pop your finger in your baby's mouth, palm up. Tickle the top of the palate with your fingertip. Most babies love a fingertip as much as a pacifier and chow down with great enthusiasm. Once your baby is fully enjoying your finger, gently pull it out and pop in the pacifier.

To maximize the benefits of pacifiers and minimize any problems:

DO BEGIN OFFERING A PACIFIER AFTER BREAST-FEEDING IS WELL ESTABLISHED. Sometimes a baby will refuse the breast after sucking on a rubber nipple. This is commonly referred to as nipple confusion. I suspect, however, there is no confusion—some babies simply prefer a rubber nipple. In order to avoid problems, a pacifier or bottle should not be introduced until the baby is well established at the breast. (I consider this to be when a baby is steadily gaining weight. In general, I advise parents to wait a minimum of 2 weeks before offering a pacifier.)

DO CHOOSE THE RIGHT PACIFIER FOR YOUR BABY. Parents often ask which pacifier is best. There is no such thing as an ideal. Some babies prefer a short nipple, while others prefer a round one. The best pacifier, then, is the one your baby prefers.

DO CHOOSE A CLEAR SILICONE PACIFIER. The yellow rubber ones tend to break down over time.

DO PAY ATTENTION TO YOUR BABY'S SIGNALS. A pacifier is meant to soothe, not silence, a baby. If your baby spits out her "binkie," it means she doesn't want it. Please don't keep sticking it back in.

DO EXPECT SOME DENTAL PROBLEMS. Prolonged or excessive pacifier use may have a detrimental effect on teeth, gums, and other dental areas. For instance, malocclusion, or "bad bite," in which the teeth are not lined up properly, is common among pacifier users.

DON'T CLEAN A PACIFIER BY STICKING IT IN YOUR MOUTH. Your saliva can easily spread germs. If the pacifier falls on the floor, rinse it under running water.

DON'T TIE OR CLIP A PACIFIER TO CLOTHING. A baby can choke or strangle, or ribbons can become twisted around tiny fingers and impair bloodflow.

DON'T DIP A PACIFIER INTO SOMETHING SWEET TO TEMPT A BABY TO TAKE IT. In particular, honey and corn syrup pose significant risks for babies because they may contain spores from the bacteria *Clostridium botulinum*. In an infant under 12 months, the spores can release a toxin that causes botulism, a life-threatening illness. Sweeteners may also cause cavities in developing teeth.

DON'T WORRY ABOUT EAR INFECTIONS. Although there's some evidence that pacifiers increase the risk of ear infections (the theory is that vigorous sucking by older babies causes a disturbance in pressure in the middle ear), the jury is still out on this one. A young baby who uses a pacifier at bedtime tends to grow into an older baby who relies on one for sleep. So, even though this study refers to older babies, it's something to keep in mind.

W: Wrap

Swaddling has been around for centuries. In the 1700s, babies were swaddled with strips of fabric because it was believed that would help limbs grow straight. Today, we swaddle for a different—and more sensible—reason: It makes a baby feel at home, which activates the sleep response.

Don't take my word for it. A study published in the journal *Pediatrics* found that swaddling increased sleep efficiency and non-rapid eye movement (non-REM) sleep. In other words, babies who were bundled slept for longer stretches.

It's no surprise young babies have so much trouble drifting off. After sleeping nestled in the womb for 9 months, suddenly a baby's world explodes. Without the snug fit of the womb, there's nothing to stop him from flailing around and smacking himself.

The good news is that it's amazingly simple to help a baby feel more secure in his new home. All it takes is a light blanket wrapped around him the right way. His limbs cooperate, his world is contained, and he feels safe. The Baby Burrito swaddle described below and shown on the opposite page is undoubtedly the best and safest swaddle.

The Baby Burrito

Pick a lightweight blanket that has some stretch to it. While flannel is cozy, it doesn't have much give. I prefer waffle-weave fabric, which is stretchy and creates a snug fit.

S: SHAPE. Fold the top point down one-quarter of the way.

W: WELCOME. Place baby on blanket with her shoulders lying on the fold. Whisper words of comfort or encouragement so she relaxes and enjoys the process.

A: ADJUST. Flex baby's arms at the elbows, and bring her hands to chest and hold them in place. This is a more natural position than having her arms restrained by her sides.

D: DRAPE. Gently wrap the right corner of the blanket over baby, and tuck it under the left buttocks and lower back.

D: DRAPE. Bring the bottom corner straight up and cover baby's arm. Tuck the edge under her body.

L: LOWER. About a hand's width from your baby's left shoulder, turn the blanket down a few inches. You only need to cover her left shoulder with this piece.

E: ENCLOSE. Holding down the piece you just turned down, gently wrap the left corner of the blanket around the baby like a belt, and secure it by folding it into itself. This last step must be done snugly to prevent it from popping open.

TIP: If you're reading this book while pregnant, don't leave the hospital without being shown how to swaddle your baby. Nurses are the best swaddlers in the world! Still confused? A great book on swaddling is *Baby-Gami: Wrapping for Beginners* by Andrea Sarvady.

Swaddling Conundrums

Should I swaddle my baby before the WOO appears?

Nurses all over the world swaddle newborns moments after birth. It keeps infants warm, comfy, and safe. As I noted in Chapter Four, you should do the same.

Why do some experts recommend swaddling with the baby's arms straight by his sides?

It's easier for a baby to sneak his arms out of the blanket if they're already partway out. Before assuming this will be a problem, however, try my method and see if it works. But if your baby is a true escape artist, able to wiggle out of the tightest swaddle like Harry Houdini, use the arms-by-the-side approach.

When should I stop swaddling?

In many modern cultures, most parents stop swaddling at 2 months—about the same time that risk of SIDS peaks (between 2 and 4 months of age). Because studies suggest that a swaddled baby more readily accepts the back-to-sleep position shown to prevent SIDS, I recommend swaddling until 3 to 4 months of age, provided your baby doesn't resist.

Do all babies need to be swaddled?

If your baby doesn't enjoy being swaddled and is a good sleeper, dozes off on her own, and stays asleep through the night, then she doesn't need to be swaddled.

What should a swaddled baby wear to bed?

I recommend only a light blanket be used. Choose appropriate jammies based on the room temperature. Typically, light clothing is best even when a light blanket is used. If you use a heavier blanket, light cotton pajamas or even just a diaper is best. To check whether your baby is overheated, slip your hand in the wrap and feel her tummy. If she's all sweaty, she's overdressed. And if her hair is damp, her cheeks are flushed, or she suffers from heat rashes, she's probably too hot.

What should the room temperature be?

To prevent overheating, keep the room a comfortable temperature between 65° and 71°F.

What if the blanket comes undone?

A loose blanket in the bed is a hazard. To keep the blanket fitting securely, use a stretchy receiving blanket (or another of comparable size) and swaddle snugly. As a rule of thumb, when you slide your hand between the blanket and your baby's chest, it should feel like you're putting your hand in the pocket of a pair of snug jeans. Test-wrap your baby during naptime so you can keep an eye on your swaddled baby.

What's the downside of swaddling?

A small percentage of babies don't enjoy it. Also, if not done properly, the swaddle can come undone, and the loose blanket could present a suffocation risk.

Other Ways to Push Your Baby's Sleep Button

In addition to the WOW! approach, there are other steps you can take to get your baby ready to sleep on her own.

BE ON TIME. Putting your baby to bed when she's tired may sound obvious—but not all babies rub their eyes or yawn to signal sleepiness. With some babies, you need to watch for more subtle clues. Here's how to read your baby's behavior and determine whether or not she's ready for sleep.

Well Rested	Tired
Happy, smiles easily	Moody, difficult to please
Feeds nicely	Fusses during feeds
Coordinated, handles self with finesse	Clumsy, uncoordinated, head seems floppier than usual
Even tempered	Giddy, moody, easily bored
Low maintenance	High maintenance
Plays happily, shows interest in what's going on, maintains focus	Futzes with ears, rubs eyes, tugs hair, arches back, sucks intensely on soother or fingers

CHOOSE THE RIGHT SLEEP LOCATION. Just as with real estate, location is everything; it has a profound influence on how a baby sleeps. Many parents keep their newborns in bassinets right next to their own beds. Initially, this isn't a problem because, as we already know, newborns do their best to block out the world. But once a baby reaches the WOO, location becomes more important.

"I decided to put a cot in the nursery because my husband is not well, and I didn't want Freddy to wake him up. This works even better than I anticipated. When Freddy begins to stir, I shush him, and he goes right back to sleep. I suspect I'm getting more sleep than I would otherwise."

—Lori, 38; Freddy, 4 months

KEEP IT CONSISTENT. Researchers at the University of Maine found that the consistency of the baby's sleep location was more important than the location itself. Playing "musical beds" (moving a child after he's fallen asleep) significantly contributed to sleep problems. Obviously, there are numerous sleeping options for you and your baby.

Baby's own room: The benefits of this choice are that you won't have to retrain your baby when you want him to sleep in the crib. Plus, he'll come to associate his bedroom with bedtime, a help when it's time to transition from crib to bed, thus warding off other sleep problems down the road. The downside is that he's not cuddled up next to you.

The traditional side bed: If you want to keep your baby within arm's reach but don't want to share your bed, this criblike bed that fits next to yours is a great alternative. See www.armsreach. com for more information. According to a new policy statement made by the American Academy of Pediatrics, a separate but close sleeping environment is recommended. Not only is a side bed a safety benefit, but it complements the Lull-a-Baby Sleeep Plan perfectly. You can sh-sh-shush your baby without even getting out of bed. The downsides (which pale in comparison to the benefits): It's another piece of baby furniture that takes up space, it's not cheap, and it doesn't convert into a crib should you decide to move your baby into

"I was worried about letting my new baby, Tyson, sleep in his own room, and I was equally worried about sleeping with him in my bed. A side bed gave me peace of mind."

—Paula, 20; Tyson, 3 years

his own room. Plus, these beds have not gone through testing by the Consumer Product Safety Commission.

The "new" side bed: I love this idea of a side bed—instead of snuggling up close with your baby in your room, you sleep in hers. Move a cot or small bed next to the crib, and enjoy the cozy comfort of sleeping next to your baby. She gets the best of both worlds: You're right there next to her, and she learns to

"Sylvia slept in her crib in our bedroom for 6 months because we live in a small house and had no other choice. Every time Sylvia made a peep, I'd pick her up and feed her. Now that she's in her own room, I can't hear her tiny sleep noises, and she seems to be sleeping for longer stretches."

—Dorothy, 39; Sylvia, 11 months

> "When Meredith reached 2 months, I moved her to her own room. Her twin brothers, now 5, slept in their own room at this age. I never had any problems with them, and I didn't want to have any problems with Meredith, either."
>
> —Siobhan, 30; Meredith, 4 months

feel comfortable in her own bed. It's easier for you to move out of her room than to move her out of yours.

Shared room: The latest studies suggest that sleeping in the same room as your baby for the first 6 months may reduce the risks of SIDS. This is different than bed sharing, because you and the baby are in separate beds. Thus, you share the benefits of being close without exposing your baby to the risks of bed sharing. Several case studies of accidental suffocation or death of undetermined cause raise concerns about bed sharing. A word of warning: Typically, the bond between you and your baby is so powerful that you will be aware of each other's movements even while asleep. But don't worry. You can deal with this by using background noise to block out sleep sounds.

In your bed: I am not going to argue the merits of bed sharing; I know that many safety-conscious parents can't resist the convenience and comfort of this choice, while other parents choose it for philosophical reasons. Whatever your beliefs, if you decide to share your bed with your baby, please, please, please respect the following safety issues.

- Young babies should go to sleep on their backs, even if cosleeping.
- Do not share your bed with your baby if you're on medication

> "Danny is my fifth child and, like each of my babies, sleeps right next to me in bed. I'm not a fanatic; keeping my kids in bed next to me is a practical choice because I need all the sleep I can get."
>
> —Magdalene, 40; Danny, 4 weeks

that makes you drowsy or if you're not sober. The risks of accidentally rolling over on your baby increase as your level of consciousness decreases. Put your baby to bed in a crib.

- Don't put your baby (or his crib, for that matter) near curtains or blinds that have a dangling draw cord.
- Never put a baby to sleep on a beanbag chair or water bed; the risk of suffocation increases on soft surfaces.
- Avoid extra bedding and pillows that can cause suffocation. (Of course, this goes for crib sleeping, too.)
- Eliminate spaces between the wall or the headboard and mattress as babies have been known to get stuck in the gap and suffocate. Don't share the bed with other children, siblings, or pets.

BED SHARING IN OTHER COUNTRIES

Although many parents argue that bed sharing is standard practice in other countries, on closer inspection, that is not entirely true. In many cultures, babies sleep next to their parents on a separate surface. For example, in Japan, babies sleep next to their mothers on a separate futon.

In the car seat, stroller, or swing: I had a mom tell me that her 3-month-old baby, Dylan, sleeps well at night in his crib, but naptime is impossible unless he's in a car seat taken into the kitchen. There, he sleeps for hours; in the crib, he only power-naps. I suggested we analyze what Dylan liked about the car seat. I suspected he slept better there because it was cozy and the room was noisy, with music blaring and his older twin siblings busy making trouble. To re-create these conditions in the bedroom, I suggested Mom swaddle Dylan and put him to bed in a bright room with loud white noise. The older kids were told they no longer needed to keep quiet. Almost immediately, Dylan began to enjoy 1- to 2-hour naps in his bed.

More Feel-Good Tips

The more relaxed your baby feels, the quicker she'll drift off to sleep. Here are a few more sweet tips to raise your baby's comfort level.

MASSAGE YOUR BABY. A recent study from Montreal found that the more infants are touched, the less they cry. So try a gentle massage before bedtime to put your baby into a relaxed frame of mind. You can find specifics in Chapter Four.

"My 11-month-old daughter, Peggy, sleeps 13 hours a night and naps for 3 hours each day. I suspect the fact that she eats like a little piggy during the day helps her make it through the night without nursing."

—Irene, 31; Peggy, 11 months

INTRODUCE YOUR BABY TO A LOVEY. Remember how passionately Linus loved his blankey and thumb? Well, more than 60 percent of kids by 1 year of age feel the same about their own "lovies." Contrary to popular belief, an attachment to a security blanket does not reflect a lack of confidence. Rather, these wonderful "buddies" facilitate autonomy and cushion the stress of bedtime separation. These attachments form at 6 months (or earlier), and the bond continues to strengthen over time.

In the past, it was recommended that a small blanket or stuffed animal be kept in the crib to encourage an attachment. But because of concerns about crib safety, it's best that a baby form a lovey attachment outside the crib until she is able to roll over both ways with ease. Once a baby is rolling over (which generally occurs around 7 months of age), she can use a blanket. To use one safely, adopt the "feet to foot" method. Place the baby in the crib with her feet close to the bottom. Choose a light blanket and tuck it in along the sides and foot of the mattress. Cover your baby with the blanket, but bring it no higher than her chest. This is safer (and different) than the typical tuck-in because Baby is placed with her feet at the bottom of the crib instead of her head at the top. This allows for a smaller blanket to be used.

If you swaddle your baby, you can later use this blanket as a lovey. In other words, the swaddle blanket eventually grows up and becomes the security blanket.

MAKE SURE BABY IS WELL FED. A baby sleeps better with a full tummy. Encourage relaxed and complete daytime feedings, and your baby will sleep better at night.

USE BEDTIME RITUALS. Stick to the same routine each night: a soothing bath, a loving massage, and a relaxed feeding. Swaddle baby, offer a pacifier, turn on white noise, say good night, and pop her in bed.

USE DAYTIME TO PERFECT SELF-CALMING TOOLS. Encourage self-calming during the daytime; it's easier on your baby to learn a new skill when he's at his best.

"The instant I put India in her crib, she grabs a handful of her 'lovey,' rubs it against her cheek, and then sleeps for 10 hours straight. I'm so proud of my great baby!"

—Nancy, 19; India, 6 months

CHAPTER EIGHT

STEP THREE: CHARM YOUR BABY INTO SLEEPY CONTENTMENT

There is no charm equal to tenderness of the heart.

—Jane Austen

In this final step, you'll learn how to charm your baby to sleep. It's that easy when you take advantage of the Window of Opportunity (WOO).

Lullabies and Battle Cries

When I trained as a midwife, we didn't have any medications to offer a mother during labor. When the intensity of her contractions overwhelmed her, we'd talk her through the pain. At one point in my training, I worked in El Paso, Texas, and the mothers who came to the midwifery clinic spoke only Spanish. I was worried: How could I talk a mom through labor if we didn't speak the same language? That's when I discovered that it wasn't what I said that comforted a laboring mother—it was how I said it. Like a disc jockey, I learned to use my voice to capture and hold an audience.

You can do the same with your voice and your baby—even before birth. In fact, researchers find that late in pregnancy, the fetal heart rate slows when Mom talks, suggesting that the baby is comforted by her voice. Right after birth, a baby turns to Mom's voice as if to say, "Mommy, is that you?"

Your voice is a powerful calming tool that makes your baby feel good, inside and out, and reliably triggers the sleep response. The reason for the ability of your voice alone to soothe your baby could be instilled in our genetic memory. An article published in *Scientific American* magazine suggested that when a Stone Age mother put her baby on the ground beside her as she foraged for food, she babbled like crazy to keep the baby quiet. A baby's cry or whisper posed a life-threatening risk of alerting enemies to their whereabouts. While modern parents don't need to worry about wild boars, the benefits of charming a baby into tranquility are also monumental.

You can also try softly singing a lullaby. The word *lullaby* comes from blending the word *lull*—"to soothe or calm"—with *bye*, as in "good-bye." Traditionally, a lullaby is a soothing song meant to help a baby fall asleep. However, although these songs are relaxing, they usually don't work unless your baby's already half asleep.

Here's how to wrap words around your baby so she feels safe and serene and succumbs to sleep.

CAPTURE YOUR BABY'S ATTENTION. If your baby is fussing, whisper softly in her ear, and she'll quiet to hear your voice. But if she's screaming, switch to a high-pitched, perky voice, and speak quickly. Once she calms, your voice should calm, too.

When you have her attention, sit close to the crib and whisper in your baby's ear "Okay, pumpkin. It's bedtime. Mommy's going to stay right by your side until you fall asleep." If your baby is fussing, keep talking . . . and talking . . . and talking.

TRY SPEAKING AT DIFFERENT TEMPOS. Some babies like you to speak slowly, like Mister Rogers, while others prefer a more upbeat tempo.

TALK LIKE A VALLEY GIRL. "It's like so-o-o late. Like totally late. You must be so-o-o tired. So like, are you ready to go to sleep?"

USE REPETITION. "Mommy loves you. Daddy loves you. Max loves you. Kori the dog loves you. Bubby loves you. Zaida loves you . . . "

Use soothing sounds especially when your baby's eyelids get heavy. "Hush-hush-hush. Hush-hush-hush."

You can record yourself and play the tape when you need a break. Put the player on louder than you normally speak, and keep it close to the crib.

Stop, Look, and Listen When Baby Cries

I can't promise you that there won't be some crying as you teach your baby to sleep. But before you panic, you need to be aware of what that crying means. Too often, when a young baby cries, parents act first and think later. They scoop the baby out of the crib,

"I was adamant that I wasn't going to let my 3-month-old twin boys cry it out, although everyone told me I had no choice. I'd heard about lulling a baby to sleep from Dr. C. At first I was reluctant to try this technique because I worried my voice would wake whichever boy fell asleep first. But right from the start, it's worked better and quicker than I imagined. First, I place the boys in separate cribs in the same room. Then I sit between the cribs and read a novel out loud. (I love to read, and until now, I was desperate for more time to read.) If one guy falls asleep before the other, I pull my chair up close to the awake one and whisper gently in his ear. Five out of six times, they fall asleep within minutes of one another. Not only have I been able to get the boys to sleep without tears, but I'm also catching up on my reading. Talk about multitasking!"

—Robin, 29; Peter and John-David, 3 months

zip down a problem list, and wonder, "Is he hungry, tired, bored, or wet?" When nothing seems to work, confusion and frustration set in.

Instead, you need to reach back to your childhood, to when you were taught how to stop, look, and listen before crossing a street. This reflective strategy teaches a child to be less impulsive and more observant and to evaluate a situation before stepping into it. Applying that strategy before going to a crying baby offers the same benefits.

If you can learn to respond rather than react to crying, you'll be better able to meet your baby's needs. My "Stop, Look, and Listen" process should take no more than a few seconds.

Although your baby might quiet down quicker if you stepped in immediately, calming your baby is not your only objective. Your major goal is to inspire your baby to soothe himself to sleep.

STOP. Hold back and take a moment to read your baby.

LOOK. Sharpen your observation skills by noting your baby's body language and facial expressions. Are your baby's hands fisted or open? Are her legs in a relaxed frog-leg position or flexed and kicking? Is her back arched or straight? Now look at her face. What color are her cheeks? What is the general impression you get when you look at your baby? Is she looking around, or are her eyes closed tight? Is she avoiding eye contact? Is she rooting? Tight fists, red face, arching back, and pumping legs say, "I need you guys!" A baby who is complaining while sucking on her toes, however, deserves the opportunity to settle herself.

LISTEN. When the WOO first opens, your baby's vocabulary is limited to three words: *wah*, *waaah*, and *waa-aaa-aaaah*. Your baby

GETTING BABIES TO SLEEP

Here are a few of the techniques the parents I worked with followed to "charm" their babies to sleep.

- After Darren put his 4-month-old son, Charles, to bed, he sat by the crib and talked about how much he loved his son: "Daddy loves you up to the sky and around the world and back again. Daddy loves you more than all the stars combined. How much does Daddy love you? More than all the creatures in the world."

- Jesse lulled her 3-month-old baby, Steffie, by speaking super slowly: "G-o-o-d n-i-g-h-t s-w-e-e-t-h-e-a-r-t. Mo-m-m-y is right h-e-r-e by your s-i-d-e."

- Steve and Tracy's 2-month-old, Emily, stayed calm when they used a monotonous tone of voice and short sentences: "Good night, pumpkin pie. Do you know what I love? Mommy loves your smile. Mommy loves your curly hair. Mommy loves your little ears. Daddy loves your pretty lips. Daddy loves your tiny toes . . . "

- Six-week-old Jen felt good when her mother read to her. Try the classic bedtime story *Goodnight Moon*, which uses repetitive prose to lull children to sleep.

- Victoria tried sweet-talking 3-month-old Eli when he fussed at naptime, but her soft-spoken voice seemed only to inflame him. His whimpering escalated to wailing, and Victoria realized that although it went against her nature, she needed to talk louder. Amazingly, as soon as she raised her voice, Eli lowered his.

whimpers when slightly upset, whines when angry, and wails when over the top. Wailing reflects a spike in emotional temperature that requires you to intervene. Otherwise, most cries all sound the same; it's just the intensity that varies. By 3 months of age, however, your baby's vocabulary expands, and it's easier to understand him.

Now, if your baby is truly upset as you try to charm him and just won't calm down, it's time for a "time-out"—which is not the same as the discipline technique used with older kids. In the Lull-a-Baby Sleep Plan, time-out is designed to be restorative. Pick up your baby and comfort him. Feed, walk, or rock your baby as long as he needs, provided he goes back into bed awake.

You can also try touching your baby to calm her down. Stroke her head, pat her tummy, or hold her hand. Don't stroke her cheek, however; you may inadvertently trigger the rooting (feeding) reflex, and she'll assume you're offering food.

TIP

Don't expect to be able to read your baby right away. Learning a new language takes time.

Another option is the TLC (Talk, Look, and Cuddle) technique we discussed with newborns. Remember?

- TALK to your baby in a perky tone.
- LOOK directly in your baby's eyes to keep him focused on you.

- CUDDLE your baby by placing him on his back, scooping your hand under his head, and picking him up by supporting his body on your forearm. Then cuddle his head in the palm of your hand at a 45-degree angle so you're looking straight into his eyes. This should help your baby calm down so you can begin charming him to sleep.

Getting tired? Call in reinforcements. Siblings can be charming, too! Older kids are amazingly talented at helping babies fall asleep (and they feel so proud when they succeed!). If an older sib wants to pitch in, have her sit with you a few times so she can absorb the basic principles. Don't expect kids to maintain their interest for long, but be sure to let them know how much you appreciate it when they help.

Also enlist Dad. Like Pavlov's dogs, babies learn to associate Mom with milk. This conditioned response makes it difficult for a baby to go to sleep when Mom is nearby because all she can think about is milk, milk, milk. The solution: Let Dad charm her to bed, and the entire process will be easier on everyone.

Common Questions about Charming a Baby to Sleep

What if my baby cries and my voice doesn't calm him down?

Learning to fall asleep is a process, and, like any process, there will be ups and downs. If your baby is stuck in a crying jag, pick him up and settle him, but once he's quiet, put him down and try again. Time spent out of the crib should be kept to a bare minimum, however, so more time can be devoted to learning the skills needed to become a sleep "self-starter." The more time spent working on self-calming skills in bed, the sooner a baby will learn to welcome sleep and drift off on his own.

Am I really supposed to talk nonstop?

Yes and no. If your baby is quiet, it's best for you to be quiet. But if she's fussing, get her attention and talk her down.

Can I sing?

While singing is soothing, it may be too stimulating. That's not good if your goal is to help a baby fall asleep, but it can work for you if you're trying to grab his attention.

When can I stop talking?

Once a baby has developed self-soothing skills, she won't need as much input from Mom or Dad. For most babies, it takes 7

WHAT ABOUT THE OTHER KIDS?

Wouldn't it be nice if you could just clone yourself, so while you're charming the 2-month-old to sleep, your clone could read a bedtime story to the 2-year-old? Obviously, that's still a dream (for now). In the meantime, try these suggestions.

- **Enlist help.** Find a teenager, grandparents, or a friend to entertain your toddler while you attend to the baby.
- **Put your older child to bed first.** That way no one feels shortchanged.
- **Share the fun.** Each adult puts one child to bed—and each child gets undivided attention.

days or less to become a sleep self-starter, provided you begin sleep training during the WOO.

Do I need to stand the whole time?

On the contrary; sit down and get comfy. Don't stand over the crib because your baby will think you're going to pick him up.

What if I sound goofy?

Don't worry if you feel self-conscious at first. Once you see how beautifully sweet-talking works, you will quickly get over your hesitation.

Isn't this teaching my baby to fall asleep only when I'm standing there?

Even the most difficult baby eventually learns to fall asleep on her own. Some babies are calmer and sleep better within days; others are more sensitive and find it difficult to settle themselves. Every baby is different.

Won't I confuse my baby by picking her up when she's fussing?

The message you send your baby is, "I'll pick you up and comfort you if you need me to, but you've got to fall asleep in your bed." Once she settles, put her back down and keep talking so she knows you're still by her side. You're not teasing your baby; you're teaching her that she can rely on you.

Aren't I teaching my baby to cry by picking her up?

If someone shows you compassion when you're upset, does it encourage you to feel upset? No! Attentiveness teaches your baby that he can depend on you.

Why does it take so long to charm a baby to sleep?

It's hard to consider the big picture when you're so tired you can't think straight. But most babies will sleep for longer stretches in 7 days (or less), provided you begin sleep training during the WOO.

How can I tell whether my baby is trying to soothe herself?
If your baby is whimpering or whining, she's self-soothing. When crying evolves into wailing, she needs your help.

$\mathscr{C}$HAPTER NINE

When Things Go Wrong

The vast majority of babies whose parents take advantage of the Window of Opportunity (WOO) will sleep for long stretches within 7 days, but there are always exceptions. Every baby is different and adjusts at his or her own speed. Really tenacious babies may need more time, more guidance, and firmer limits. Please don't give up! Stick with me on this—I guarantee things will get better.

Overcoming Glitches

So you're following the Lull-a-Baby Sleep Plan to the letter, but your baby still isn't falling asleep on his own or sleeping through the night? Here are the two main glitches I hear about from parents.

GLITCH #1: HE WON'T FALL ASLEEP WITHOUT MY HELP! Be consistent no matter what. Babies are so smart that if you give them the slightest impression that it pays to cry, they'll do so relentlessly. Send a crystal-clear message—"I love you dearly, but you must go to sleep in your crib"—and your baby will adjust. And follow the Lull-a-Baby Golden Rule: Your baby needs to fall asleep in bed. If you sometimes allow him to fall asleep in your arms during a feeding, he will hold out for this every time. Although he may be tiny, his will-power is not.

> Every night I start the bedtime routine full of optimism. I promise myself 'tonight will be different.' But after listening to Lorian fuss for 10 minutes, I typically cave in. I scoop him out of bed and rock him to sleep. Every night I tell myself the same thing—I'll do better tomorrow. But Lorian knows full well I'll rock him to sleep if he keeps crying . . . and he's right!
> —*Freda, 36; Lorian, 7 months*

GLITCH #2: SHE KEEPS WAKING UP IN THE NIGHT. When a baby isn't sleeping through the night, I ask Mom and Dad three key questions.

- How does your baby fall asleep?
- What happens when she wakes up?
- Are you consistent in how you help your baby fall asleep?

While it's very common for a baby to wake during the night, before assuming you need to feed her, see if you can charm her back to sleep. If so, then she's not hungry. If not, offer a quick feeding, and then put her back in bed sleepy-awake.

When a young baby—4 months old or younger—has mastered fall-ing asleep but continues to wake during the night, it's fair to assume he's waking up because he's hungry, even if he weighs more than 12 pounds. Four to 6 months of age is a gray area. Although most 12-pound babies can sleep for longer stretches during the night, some get hungry earlier. Obviously, babies are human beings and need to be treated as individuals.

After 6 months of age, however, night awakenings reflect habit, not hunger. Therefore, if your baby is still waking, phase out night feedings using one of the supergentle methods below.

There are two basic approaches for weaning a baby off night feedings: the fast and the slow. During the WOO, both usually work equally well, but some babies are better suited to one approach over the other. You're the best judge of the right approach for your baby.

The Fast Route: This involves lulling your baby back to sleep when he wakes up during a 9-hour stretch. Although it may seem abrupt, some babies adapt quicker with this approach because of its absolute message: "Go to sleep. It's bedtime."

The quickest way to tell the little guy the all-night diner is closed is to stop feeding him for up to 9 hours. Give your baby a "dream nosh" just before you go to bed, and you'll both benefit. Having just given your baby a top-off, you won't need to worry about him being hungry when he wakes up crying, and you'll get more sleep if the blessed 9 hours begins when you go to bed.

When you're ready to call it a night, gently scoop your baby out of bed and put him to the breast. Nurse him for a few minutes, and then pop him back in bed. If you're bottle-feeding, you can simply prop your baby up and feed him without removing him from the crib. Most babies are so groggy that they don't fully wake up, and this feeding becomes a lovely dream.

What happens later in the night? When your baby wakes up, you follow the Lull-a-Baby Sleep Plan and make every effort to ease him into sleep without taking him out of the crib. Pat him on the back, adjust his position, shush-shush-shush, and reassure him—but don't feed him. If you absolutely must, take your baby out of the crib and comfort him, as long as you put him back in bed sleepy-awake.

Babies have enormous stamina and can outlast you without tiring. Therefore, it's best to share this supportive role. If you find yourself losing momentum, remember—sleep is crucial to your baby's health.

The Slow Route: With this method, you wean your baby off night feeds by incrementally reducing the time spent at the breast or bottle. If your baby is bottle-feeding, provide him with less milk with each feeding until he's eventually down to nothing.

If she's breastfeeding, gradually decrease feeding times. Let's say your baby tends to suckle for 15 minutes. Keep feedings closer to 10 minutes for the next few nights. Slowly withdraw your nipple from your infant's mouth and cuddle her before placing her back in the crib. What if she resists? Do a remake. Put your baby back to the breast, and after a few moments try to take your nipple out of her mouth. Keep repeating this step until she stops pining for the breast.

Each night cut feeding time down by a minute until you reach 3 minutes. Most babies will stop waking up for feedings at this point because they've slowly become accustomed to guiding themselves back to sleep. From start to finish, this process should take no longer than 10 days.

Defining "Sleeping through the Night"

Those four tiny words mean entirely different things to different people. Some experts use the term to suggest a baby will sleep for 5 to 6 hours at a stretch, while others promise 12 hours.

But your baby is not a statistic; she's an individual with her own needs and norms. I suggest, then, that we define "sleeping through the night" in individual terms. A baby who sleeps through the night goes to bed at night and doesn't get up until morning. The total number of hours slept depends on a baby's nature, needs, and nurturing.

Major Mistakes Made with the Lull-a-Baby Sleep Plan

In this section, you'll learn how to identify and quickly fix mistakes. Luckily, success doesn't require a medical degree or previous experience. All you need is the ability to stand back and objectively consider your situation.

Once identified, most problem areas can be fixed with a few simple modifications. The following checklist includes the most commonly committed sleep mistakes and their simple solutions during the WOO. Please read through the entire list; most sleep mistakes are not isolated problems.

The Pacifier Trap

THE PROBLEM: As I've explained, the pacifier is a mixed blessing. It helps a baby relax and eases him into sleep, but at the same time, it becomes a crutch a baby depends on to fall asleep. If he loses his pacifier in his sleep, he'll wake up and cry out for you to pop it back in—every few hours.

THE FIX: According to the latest research, a pacifier may help reduce the risk of sudden infant death syndrome (SIDS). Experts aren't sure just how it helps, but some theorize that a pacifier makes a baby more sensitive to arousing if he encounters breathing problems during the night. Here's how to reap the benefits while sidestepping the drawbacks: Offer your baby a pacifier at bedtime. If he spits it out, don't keep popping it back in. Now, the most important point: Don't give your baby a pacifier when he wakes up during the night. The literature does not suggest there are any benefits in reducing SIDS by using a pacifier during the night—but from a sleep-learning perspective, there are clear disadvantages in doing so.

Timing Troubles

THE PROBLEM: If you put your baby to bed when she's either overtired or not sleepy, you're going to run into problems. Many parents put off bedtime because they believe a baby who's about to crash will fall asleep more readily. Unfortunately, that assumption is entirely wrong. An overtired baby doesn't have the reserves needed to soothe herself to sleep and will typically shriek once she finds herself in bed. On the flip side, if you put a baby who's not even remotely tired to bed, it stands to reason that she won't nod off—she'll fuss and cry until you pick her up.

THE FIX: Get your timing right. If it's hard to read your baby's body language, err on the side of safety and put him to bed a tad earlier than you are now. As a rule of thumb, during the WOO, young babies tend to need a nap midmorning and a second in the afternoon and will sleep for about 12 hours at night. Watch for signs of fatigue as described on page 92 and pop him in his bed before he gets a second wind.

Thumb-Sucking Dilemmas

THE PROBLEM: When a thumbsucker can't find her thumb, she won't sleep well.

THE FIX: Thumb sucking is a powerful soothing tool that's always there when your baby needs to relax. According to an informal study I carried out in my office last year, a thumbsucker is twice as likely to sleep through the night as a pacifier user. Your nights will get much easier once your baby's thumb becomes accessible. She'll develop the skills she needs for thumb sucking around 3 months of age. Some babies are born thumbsuckers, others are not. Don't put mittens on her hands that might interfere with her ability to get her thumb into her mouth. If you're worried about Baby scratching herself, file her nails so there are no sharp edges.

Swaddling Conundrums

THE PROBLEM: Some parents continue to swaddle past the point where their baby actually enjoys it.

THE FIX: Stop swaddling if your baby is sucking his thumb; at the very least, swaddle but leave out one arm. Most babies are ready to give up swaddling by 3 to 4 months.

Room Sharing

THE PROBLEM: While sharing your room with your infant is lovely, reassuring, and possibly even protective against SIDS, it often leads to more frequent night awakenings. Babies grunt, groan, and squeak when sleeping lightly. If you pick your baby up whenever she's in a light sleep state, she won't learn how to fall back into a deeper sleep. If your baby hears you tossing and turning when she's in a light sleep, she's more likely to cry out.

THE FIX: Don't jump up and pick up your baby at the slightest complaint. Use white noise to minimize sounds that might distract your baby when he's in the same room as you. By 6 months of age, move your baby into his own room.

Hot, Hot, Hot

THE PROBLEM: Many babies are bundled too heavily for bed. It's harder to sleep when you're sweltering; plus, overdressing may interfere with the role your baby's body temperature plays in the sleep/wake cycles.

THE FIX: It's better to be a little too cold than a little too hot. Keep the room at a temperature where you would feel comfortable when lightly dressed.

Props Posing a Problem

THE PROBLEM: Your baby has become accustomed to certain conditions for falling asleep and requires them to doze off after a brief night awakening, as well.

THE FIX: Don't use any props to help your baby fall asleep that won't be there when he wakes up during the night. The exception to this rule is a pacifier, which can be given at the beginning of the night but shouldn't be popped back in once it's spit out. Leave white noise on all night until your baby cultivates falling-asleep skills.

Asleep to Bed

THE PROBLEM: Your baby isn't going to bed awake and learning how to doze off on her own, so she wakes up whenever she's in a light sleep.

THE FIX: Put your baby to bed sleepy-awake so she can practice and perfect her falling-asleep skills. This point is crucial to your success.

Falling Asleep at the Breast/Bottle

THE PROBLEM: Suckling is so relaxing that it puts your baby right to sleep—before you put her into bed.

THE FIX: Feed your baby earlier in the evening so he doesn't fall asleep while suckling.

Crying the Blues?

THE PROBLEM: Nothing is worse than just standing back and listening to your baby cry.

THE FIX: Some babies won't develop self-calming skills unless pushed to do so. Give your baby an opportunity to settle himself before intervening on his behalf. Naturally, if your baby can't settle himself, you should step in and offer comfort—but stop, look, and listen before rushing to the rescue.

No Schedule

THE PROBLEM: Your baby doesn't have a regular schedule and, hence, can't get to sleep when it's bedtime.

THE FIX: The more predictable your baby's schedule, the fewer sleep problems you're likely to encounter. If a schedule does not naturally evolve by the time a baby is 3 months old, you need to encourage one. Try the Up-Down-Up-Down Routine.

Up: After your baby sleeps, pick him up and feed him.
Down: After you feed him, put him down and let him play. Depending on the age of your baby, this period will last anywhere from an hour (6 weeks to 2 months old) to 3 or 4 hours (2 months and older). If you have

errands and need to run around, this is the time to do it.

Up: Pick up your baby again and feed him when it's nearly naptime or bedtime.

Down: Now put him in bed to sleep.

Here's how a typical morning might look, given that most mothers are racing against the clock.

6:00 AM: Baby starts to squirm and makes waking sounds. You stay put in the hope she'll fall back to sleep.

6:30 AM: Quiet noises become piercing wails. You pick your baby up, change her diaper, dress her, and enjoy a relaxing feeding.

7:00 AM: You have an hour to get your preschooler fed, dressed, and ready for daycare. So your baby goes down on the floor to play, which you hope will last long enough to get your other child ready.

8:00 AM: It's your girlfriend's turn to take the kids to school, so you have a little extra time. You keep Baby entertained as you drink some coffee, dress quickly, tidy the kitchen, and throw in a load of laundry. You need to pick the kids up from daycare, so you want to get Baby down for a nap so she'll be up and ready by noon.

9:30 AM: Baby is getting antsy and can't be easily distracted. You pick her up, feed her, and change her diaper.

10:00 AM: It's naptime. You put Baby down in her crib and stand ready to lull her to sleep.

11:30 AM: Baby wakes after a good nap. You scoop her up and give her a quick feeding, and you're out the door by noon.

And so on. . . .

Up-Down-Up-Down represents portions of the day divided into Eat/
Up, Play/Down, Eat/Up, Sleep/Down chunks. In the morning
there's one Up-Down-Up-Down cycle, and in the afternoon another.
It's best to plan errands during the time devoted to play, as your baby
will be at her best during this time.

Sending Mixed Messages

THE PROBLEM: Your baby cries after you've put him to bed, so you
scoop him out and then feed, jiggle, or rock him to sleep—essentially,
teaching him to cry.

THE FIX: Send your baby a clear message: After you put him to bed,
guide him to fall asleep using the Lull-a-Baby Sleep Plan. Be nearby
to offer reassurance with your voice, and provide time out of the crib
if needed. But this part is nonnegotiable: Put your baby back in the
crib sleepy-awake.

$\mathscr{C}$HAPTER TEN

BRIDGING THE NAP GAP

When should I stop giving my kids a nap?

—Mother of three children under age 5

When you don't need them anymore!

—Ann Landers

I'm sure I don't need to tell you why the curtain needs to come down once or twice a day to allow for a baby's nap. Aside from the obvious reasons—you have laundry to fold, bills to pay, and e-mails to answer—there is a more important consideration. Naps are critical for growing minds and bodies.

Naps give the brain a chance to process the events of the day while providing a chance to recharge (for both you *and* your baby). Studies find that babies who nap well have longer attention spans and are less fussy than poor nappers. And although this next point seems counterintuitive, babies who nap well during the day sleep better at night. Naps are also a precious opportunity for your baby to work on self-calming skills.

Even adults can benefit from naps; research finds that we naturally feel groggy between 1:00 and 3:00 PM. That's when our productivity, dexterity, and mental sharpness suffer. But power naps provide numerous restorative benefits, reducing burnout while increasing performance and learning. So stop feeling guilty about napping!

The Window of Opportunity to Establish Healthy Naps

Once your baby "wakes up" to the wonders of the world, where, when, and how naps occur matters enormously. But just how do naptime routines differ from bedtime?

They don't. The same strategies should be used day and night. Sometimes, however, I find *more* white noise is needed to help a baby calm down at naptime. When a baby naps, she keeps one ear cocked to make sure she doesn't miss out on anything. Loud white noise masks these sounds and allows her to zone out.

Napping Schedule		
Age	**Number of naps**	**Length of nap**
2–18 months	2 (after breakfast and lunch)	½–2 hours
18–24 months	1 (usually after lunch)	1–2 hours
2–4 years	1 (midafternoon)	1–1½ hours

Since naps are precious, they need to be safeguarded. Here are simple ways to protect naptime.

DON'T KEEP LATE NIGHTS. If your baby goes to bed late at night, it interferes with an early morning nap. Stick to an early evening bedtime, even if it means putting your baby to bed before your spouse is home from work.

ACT FAST. When your baby looks and acts tired, it's best to put him right to bed. If you first take the time to make a quick call, put the dog in the backyard, and throw a load of laundry in the dryer, he may find a second wind and skip the nap. Your baby is ready to have a nap if he demonstrates some of the following behaviors.

- Acts giddier or goofier than usual
- Loses interest in playing
- Just wants to be held
- Lies down without encouragement
- Yawns, rubs eyes, sucks on thumb or pacifier while staring into space
- Wants to suckle
- Loses balance easily
- Avoids eye contact
- Has glazed look

Unlike adults, tired babies become hyper and giddy. The more tired the baby, the more wound up she gets. As you can imagine, it's harder to charm a wired baby to sleep than a tired one.

Peter, father of 6-month-old Faye, learned this lesson the hard way. After Mom would go off to work, Peter and Faye would eat breakfast together and then go for a stroll. Inevitably, Faye would fall asleep in her stroller before they would make it to the end of the first block. She'd stay asleep until they got home and wake up with a smile. But the afternoon nap was another story entirely.

"Faye fights to keep her eyes open, although she's totally miserable," says Peter. "She's exhausted, but that doesn't stop her from hollering bloody murder when she's put in her crib. I've tried tiring Faye out, but the later I keep her up, the harder she is to put down."

KEEP IT CONSISTENT. Napping at the same time every day helps set your baby's body clock so she's ready for a nap at the same time every day.

STAY AWAY FROM BAD HABITS. Some parents tell me, "The only way my baby will nap is if I lie down with her." Before you allow ineffective habits to form, ask yourself, "Do I really want to be doing this in the days, weeks, months, and possibly years to come?"

The Seven Most Common Nap Traps

Have you been tripped up by any of these situations?

NAP TRAP #1: "MY BABY WAKES UP THE INSTANT I PUT HIM DOWN." He shouldn't fall asleep in your arms in the first place. Remember the rule: *to bed semi-awake.*

NAP TRAP #2: "MY BABY REFUSES TO NAP." Typically, the problem is timing. A baby won't nap unless he's tired. Try too early, and he'll resist; try too late, and he'll catch a second wind. In general, a young baby needs to nap after 2 hours of activity.

NAP TRAP #3: "MY BABY TAKES ONLY SHORT NAPS." There are several equally good reasons a baby may take only catnaps. First, a short nap may be all she needs; some babies are fully energized after 30 to 40 minutes of sleep. But this next reason is more likely the culprit: Your baby may be having problems going from a shallow to a deep sleep state. She may wake up after 20 minutes because she can't settle down. Here are some ways to help your baby relax.

- TURN DOWN THE VOLUME.
  Remember, it takes 10 to 20 minutes for a young baby to fall into a deep sleep. You must proceed with caution during the transition. The fewer distractions, the greater the likelihood he'll nod off. Young babies sleep best surrounded by white noise, but sometimes loud, sudden household noises interfere with drifting off. If there are older siblings at home, consider using white noise to minimize outside distractions. Like the mantra "om . . . om . . . om . . .," white noise allows a baby to dive into a deeper level of consciousness. Once he's asleep, there's no need to keep the troops quiet.

- GET THERE FIRST.
  If your baby consistently wakes up after a 30-minute nap, tiptoe into her room around the 20-minute mark, and charm her back to sleep once she starts the wake-up shuffle. Don't leave the room before she's in a deep sleep (see page 5). If you try to sneak out too early, she'll notice and wake up.

- THINK OUTSIDE THE CRIB.
  Even when your baby's sleeping, his gifted brain is busy soaking up outside signals. A dark room sends the message "go back to sleep" and can extend naptime. So hang dark curtains, and get rid of the night-light.

NAP TRAP #4: "MY BABY NAPS BEST IN HER CAR SEAT." A baby who loves to sleep in her car seat is most likely one who loves to feel cuddled, as though she's in a cocoon—which isn't surprising, considering a baby spends 9 months curled up in the womb.

Swaddling is the best way to re-create this comfort. According to recent studies, swaddling helps babies sleep longer.

NAP TRAP #5: "MY BABY POWER-NAPS IN THE CAR ON THE WAY HOME FROM DAYCARE AND THEN REFUSES TO GO TO BED." Some things can't be helped, but that doesn't mean you shouldn't try. Here are some suggestions: Ask your daycare provider to record your baby's naps for a week. Play around with the timing of the afternoon nap so he's not so tired when you pick him up. Avoid giving your baby a bottle on the way home—the moving car plus relaxed sucking is a dangerous duo. Finally, when choosing a daycare center, consider one close to home so you can at least try to reduce the risk of your baby falling asleep on the way home.

NAP TRAP #6: "MY BABY ONLY CATNAPS BECAUSE WE'RE ALWAYS ON THE GO." Some families are so busy that it's hard to squeeze in a good nap. There's nothing intrinsically wrong with short naps, as long as your baby is well rested. However, if your baby falls apart at the end of the day, is hard to please, dozes off the instant he's in the car seat, or is high maintenance, I'd rethink your activities. If you have an older child with a jam-packed schedule, perhaps it's time to simplify. In an effort to allow stay-at-home naptime, I suggest you cut back on commitments, carpool, or hire a sitter.

NAP TRAP #7: "MY BABY WILL NAP ONLY IF I LIE DOWN WITH HER." There is nothing wrong with lying down with your baby, provided you're prepared to do this for a long time; it's the kind of habit that's hard to break. Instead, sit beside her bed and charm her to sleep. She'll feel the same sense of closeness and ultimately sleep for longer stretches. Best of all, you can sneak out of the room as she becomes more adept at self-soothing to sleep.

Why Babies Resist Naps

One mother once told me she spent her entire day trying to get her 5-month-old daughter to nap somewhere other than the car. I asked a few probing questions and soon realized why this mom was having so many problems. Little Lilly stayed up until 10:00 PM every night so she could see her father when he got home from work. She never had a morning nap because she slept in. By early afternoon, Lilly was overtired, so she power-napped in the car on the way to pick up her brother from preschool.

Her second nap occurred around dinnertime, when she crashed in the wind-up swing while her mom prepared dinner. Ultimately, all the sleep problems stemmed from Lilly staying up late to play with Dad. When she was given an earlier bedtime, the naps naturally fell into place.

Here are some other common reasons babies resist naps.

- NOT TIRED.
  A baby needs to be tired before she'll take a nap. While babies tend toward regular naptimes, it's best to keep one eye on the clock and the other on your baby. Some days your baby will be tired a little earlier; sometimes, a little later. Let your baby dictate the best time for a nap, but strive to keep it consistent, give or take 10 minutes.
- TOO MANY DISTRACTIONS.
  Initially, a newborn thrives on noise and activity when he's trying to sleep. But by about 3 months, a noisy environment is a distraction and interferes with falling asleep.

- OVERTIRED.

   Babies handle being overtired differently than adults do. An overtired baby has difficulty calming down and falling asleep. It's like trying to get shut-eye when taking the red-eye; you may be dead tired, but you can't sleep.

- MEDICATIONS.

   Any over-the-counter cold and allergy preparations and asthma medications mom has taken can transfer into breast milk, stimulating the baby and interfering with her ability to fall asleep and stay asleep.

- TEETHING.

   A baby may be able to distract himself from teething — discomfort during daytime activities, but alone in his bed, it's all he can think about. However, be careful not to blame teething too often—it's a handy culprit but rarely the root of the problem. (For more on teething, see page 187.)

Naptime Is *Not* Bedtime

At naptime a baby wakes up and stays up—while at night, a baby who wakes up is expected to go back to sleep. How's a tiny baby supposed to grasp such subtleties?

Easily! If you emphasize the difference, your baby will catch on.

For instance, when you pick your baby up after a nap, use a singsong voice and say, "Good morning [or afternoon], sunshine"; turn on the lights; and stroke, hug, and cuddle her. At night, keep the room dark and quiet. Don't say a word if she wakes in the night, and keep cuddles to a minimum. If you must say anything, whisper.

If you emphasize the contrast between day and night sleeping, your baby will soon learn the difference.

Finally, perhaps my most important advice: Please, take advantage of the nap! Set a good example for your baby and use the time to rest yourself. The mother of one of my patients, Penelope, used to laugh to herself when her friends said, "Sleep when the baby sleeps." She'd whisper under her breath, "Yeah, right. And leave my 18-month-old to fend for herself?" But when Penelope fell down a flight of stairs and ended up in a full leg cast, she managed the impossible. Every day she put both kids down for a nap at the same time and spent an hour on the couch resting. Nowadays she reminds herself, "Never say 'never'."

CHAPTER ELEVEN

OPPORTUNITY KNOCKS TWICE

Convincing your older baby to change her sleep habits can be more challenging than trying not to push when the baby's head is crowning. Yet both are possible. If you approach this mission thoughtfully and understand what an older baby needs to fall asleep, most night fights can be avoided.

After the Window of Opportunity (WOO) closes, babies have formed deep-rooted falling-asleep habits. This makes sleep training more difficult, because ineffective habits need to be broken before new ones can be formed. But the great news is that as one window closes, another opens. Although you've missed the WOO, the unique talents of older babies hold new promise. An older, more mature night owl has more intellectual and physical tools at her disposal.

Before we get down to specifics, I would like to touch on one of the least recognized and most valuable incentives for change—*frustration*.

Frustration: The Crucial Ingredient for Transforming Your Night Owl's Sleep Habits

Many parents fail at sleep training because of a fundamental misunderstanding about what it takes to succeed. Exhausted parents want babies to adopt new habits without resisting—but a human baby is a tough fighter. He can cry louder and longer than you or I, and he can hold his breath till he's blue in the face or passes out. Like a butterfly that boosts its strength by struggling out of its chrysalis, a baby needs to learn to work through frustration in order to benefit from it.

Consider the not-quite-crawling baby who wants a toy that's out of reach. As she tries to get the desired object, her frustration grows and grows until she can't take it anymore. She starts to wiggle around, grunt, and groan, and the next thing you know, she's crawling.

The same thing happens when you put your baby in his crib awake. At first, he may cry as if to say, "Excuse me, people, but aren't you forgetting something? You're supposed to rock me to sleep!" But a few moments later, he's looking for ways to soothe himself. The idea that a touch of frustration is good for your baby may seem ludicrous—but it's true.

Of course, when your baby *needs* you, you should attend to her immediately. But not every cry is a code blue. The trick is to differentiate between a cry that says "I *need* you mommy!" and one that says "I *want* you mommy!" Needs and wants are different!

In order to take advantage of an older baby's new talents, you need to be aware of what they are.

MOTOR SKILLS. Older babies can sit up and maneuver their way around the crib. They can squirm, flip-flop, or rock themselves to sleep. They can pull themselves up and sit themselves down. And they can wiggle around until they find a comfortable position that helps them fall asleep. They can pop their own pacifiers back in their mouths. Alas, an older baby can also stand up, holler "Mommy, Mommy!" and shake the rails of the crib until they come loose.

VISION. Older babies see things in three dimensions and color and can recognize you clear across the room. If you pop your head in the door, your baby is aware of you, even if the room is dark. And now that the world is in focus, Baby can unwind with a good book, stare at the sky, or contemplate shapes and shadows.

HEARING. By 6 months, your baby's hearing is as developed as an adult's is. Plus, your baby has developed a memory for sounds and will be comforted by a familiar song or voice. Here's how a Bubby I know took advantage of this tool to guide her grandbaby to sleep: "My grandchild Randy, 11 months old, loves it when I sing 'Twinkle, Twinkle, Little Star.' Although my daughter complains he's a lousy sleeper, when Randy sleeps over at my house, I sing a few rounds of his favorite song, and he drifts off to sleep."

COMMUNICATION SKILLS. Your baby is stringing vowels and consonants together. Facial expressions and gesturing are now evident. Although your baby has no words, her moods are clearly expressed. She's learned to get your attention in a variety of ways outside of crying. Not only is your older baby easier to read but, with a new level of communicability, she's better able to read you, too. This is really good news because it means you don't need to worry that sleep training will hurt her psyche. Your smart baby understands that you adore her even if she doesn't get her way.

INTELLECTUAL DEVELOPMENT. By 6 months of age, your baby has grasped the concept that an object exists even when it's out of his sight. That means he knows that when you walk out of his room, you'll return. Your older baby is equipped to play by himself, which is a great way to relax before drifting off to sleep. Plus, when you sleep-train an older baby, his brain catches on quickly.

SOCIAL INTERACTIONS. Although your baby loves your attention, she's beginning to enjoy her own company, too. She'll entertain herself before falling asleep and is more adept at self-comforting.

Before we delve into specific needs of older babies, let's revisit some general sleep routines that encourage babies, big and little, to fall (and stay) asleep.

1. RELAXING RITUALS. Help your baby unwind with a soothing bedtime routine, such as: yummy dinner, quiet playtime, toasty bath, loving massage, warm milk, favorite lullaby—and then it's good night.
2. RESCHEDULED FEEDINGS. If your baby is in the habit of nursing to sleep, I suggest you feed him earlier so he doesn't fall asleep at the breast.
3. MORE NAPS. A good nap encourages a good night's rest. In fact, the more a baby sleeps during the day, the more she'll sleep at night, provided the naps occur at a reasonable hour, such as early afternoon.
4. PROPER TIMING. Watch your baby, not the clock, and put her to bed at the first sign of fatigue. Don't wait for your pip-squeak to crash.

Pushing an Older Baby's Sleep Button

In Chapter Seven, I described how to push a young baby's sleep button by providing him with conditions similar to those in the womb and using the WOW steps. Older babies, however, need a different set of ingredients to help them sleep.

A SLEEP NEST. Remember Pavlov's discovery of the phenomenon he called the conditioned reflex? An older baby has a terrific memory and will come to associate her crib with falling asleep if given the chance.

A LOVEY. Now that your baby has more sophisticated social skills, he can form a loving bond with a sleep buddy—a special blanket, teddy, or other stuffed animal. And nothing, *absolutely nothing,* helps a baby snooze like a sleep buddy. How do you encourage the attachment? Like a good matchmaker, you introduce your baby to a special blanket or stuffed animal and provide them with plenty of opportunity to mingle. Give your baby the same blanket or stuffed animal to snuggle with whenever she fusses, and put it in the crib every night. Keep only one small crib-safe lovey handy. If you're lucky, a bond will form and strengthen with time.

OUT OF SIGHT, OUT OF MIND. Put your baby's favorite toys in a toy box so he isn't tempted by them when he's trying to sleep.

DISCOVERY OF THE SLEEP BUTTON. Do you remember when your baby was about 2 months old and discovered her hands and

---

TIP

The crucial point here is that to form an effective learned reflex linking crib and sleep, your baby needs to fall asleep in bed— not in your arms.

---

couldn't stop staring at them? Later she discovered her toes and sucked on them enthusiastically: "Wow! I didn't know I had such yummy toes." These discoveries came about through a process of self-exploration. Well, babies find their sleep button through a similar self-discovery process. They wiggle around, suck on their fingers and toes, and babble away until they let go and drift off to Z-z-z Land. The more they practice, the more adept they become.

In the following section, you're going to learn how to tap into your older baby's newfound talents to help him lose ineffective habits and discover his precious sleep button.

The Sticky Wicket: Undoing Bad Habits

So how do you undo ineffective sleep habits without becoming undone yourself? Recall that the sleep habits a baby is exposed to during the WOO are stored in her memory bank. These habits are the only falling-asleep experience a baby knows. As you can imagine, breaking those habits can be tricky and takes time, tenacity, and tact.

Changing those habits is like forcing a right-handed person to use the left hand—it's challenging, frustrating, confusing, and exhausting but somehow doable. A baby is equally strong—he may be small in size, but he's big in potential! But change takes time, and time takes patience. You will need both.

So, after you finish your bedtime routine, put your older baby in bed semi-awake. Presumably, this is *not* how she's accustomed to falling asleep, so expect some degree of resistance; a little petunia may whimper, while an angry tiger will roar. Your top job is to H.E.L.P. your baby discover the skills she already possesses to fall asleep by simultaneously providing the support she needs to feel safe and the space she needs to grow. Here's how.

H = Hang back

E = Empathize

L = Love

P = Persevere

Hang Back

If your older baby begins to cry, your first course of action is to hang
back. An older baby possesses the mental and physical abilities to
deal with frustration. He can wiggle around until he feels comfortable and stay calm now that he's more aware, confident, and capable.
You already know that frustration serves as motivation for change,
and that's why you need to give your baby wiggle room to grow and
learn. He's got all the tools he needs to soothe himself; he just needs
encouragement to use them.

There are no hard-and-fast rules about how long to hang back.
If your baby is enjoying her own company, there's no reason to

step in. If she's wailing and you've already held back a few minutes, it's time to go to her. However, give her one last chance before intervening. Count to 60, and if your baby is still crying, lend a hand.

Empathize

Your big, smart baby is well equipped to soothe himself to sleep. He has intellectual and social know-how, and his motor skills are top-notch. But he may need a nudge from you to get the process going. Your baby has learned that crying gets your attention, and he expects you to show up when he's upset. There is no reason to interfere with this sense of trust, but when you respond to tears, come with understanding and empathy instead of milk and cuddles.

You wouldn't let your toddler play with a sharp knife, no matter how loud she cried. You'd say something like, "I'm sorry, sweetheart, but it's not a toy." She could cry until she was blue in the face, and you still wouldn't let her play with it. Well, directing your baby toward healthy sleep habits should be approached with an equally firm but loving response: "I know you're upset, but it's bedtime." Your tiny baby may not understand the meaning of your words, but he'll understand the tone of your voice. Use an empathetic but firm tone of voice, and your baby will get the message: "I love you, but it's bedtime."

> When my daughter, Nadia, was 9 months old, I went down South to visit my mother. My husband couldn't take the time off, so I went without him. My husband hated it when Nadia cried, even a little, so we'd waltz around the room with her in our arms until she conked out. But my mother was shocked when she saw how I put Nadia to bed and asked, "Why don't you just put her down when she's tired?"
> "I don't want her to cry," I said.
> The next day at naptime, my mother asked, "Can I put Nadia to bed? I promise I won't let her cry." She put Nadia in her crib and pulled up a chair and sat next to her. My mother read the paper as Nadia sucked on her fingers, wiggled about, and talked to herself. As soon as Nadia began to whine, my mother whispered, "Sh-sh-sh. Go to sleep." I would never have believed it if I didn't see for myself, but Nadia fell asleep without making a peep. The next day, I asked my mother to put Nadia down for a nap, and the same thing happened. By the time I returned home, Nadia was falling asleep on her own, sleeping through the night, and waking up with a magnificent smile on her face.
> —*Marta L., 28; Nadia, 9 months*

Empathizing means providing your baby with kind words instead of cuddles. You're her support person, not her solution. The goal is to support your baby through the self-discovery process until she discovers how to fall asleep on her own. Gail, a professional gymnastics coach, wasn't thrilled about letting 10-month-old Nina cry but couldn't stand the thought of another night without sleep. She decided to do what she does best: coach her. Gail put Nina in her crib awake and then sat next to her and provided encouragement and comfort from the sidelines until Nina fell asleep.

But what if your baby won't stop wailing? Let's say he's worked himself into a frenzy, and your reassuring words are drowned out by his glass-shattering screams. Well, forgive me for repeating myself, but this next point is so important it bears repeating: *As one Window of Opportunity closes, another one opens.* An older baby has many tools, both physical and mental, at his disposal to overcome stress. He's developed the concept of permanence, which means he knows you'll come back into his room sooner or later. He's socially astute and realizes you love him, even if you don't run to the rescue the instant he cries. But sometimes babies, especially sensitive ones, need more support to help them fall asleep. Unlike new babies, they don't need distractions like swaddling, suckling, and shushing; they just need you. So if your baby is miserable, go into his room and cheer him up.

Love

Comfort your baby. If she needs a snuggle, scoop her up and give her one. Most likely, she'll settle down the moment she sees you. That's good—but how are you ever going to get out of the room again? The following strategy is designed to reassure your baby with your presence yet acclimatize her to being alone in the crib. I call it the "Oops, I'll Be Right Back" method.

After comforting your baby, pop him back in the crib and say, "Oops. Mommy forgot something. I'll be right back!" I know your baby doesn't understand your words, but trust me; he'll catch on pretty quickly.

Walk out of the room. Stay out for a minute or longer if you can bear it. When you return, if your baby is crying, do whatever is necessary to calm him down. Lift him out of the crib, feed him, jiggle him . . . then put him back in his crib semi-awake.

Now it's time for another round. Say, "Oops. Mommy has to do something. I'll be right back!" Stay away a little longer each time. This way you give your baby a gentle nudge to settle himself before you return. If he cries when you leave, say, "It's okay, pumpkin. Mommy's coming back. I'll be back in a jiffy." One of these times, your little guy will fall asleep while you're out of the room.

Continue this in-and-out routine for as long as it takes for your baby to fall asleep. Think "short-term pain, long-term gain."

Persevere

The Lull-a-Baby Sleep Plan is designed to gently persuade your baby toward healthier sleep habits. Because our goal is to make the process as painless as possible, the trade-off is time. It takes longer to walk a mile than to run it, but either way, you reach the finish line. Walking, however, is easier on the system, which is crucial for those of us who are out of shape. The same thing can be said of H.E.L.P.-ing your baby develop more effective sleep habits: It may take longer, but it hurts less.

Remember Aesop's fable "The Tortoise and the Hare"? The hare boasts about his speed and challenges anyone to race him. The tortoise accepts the challenge, which the hare assumes is a big joke. The race is set, and the two take off. The tortoise slowly plods along while the hare arrogantly decides to take a nap, believing he can catch up anytime. But he oversleeps, only to wake up and see the tortoise crossing the finish line.

Like the tortoise, you need to hang in during sleep training because slow but steady wins the race. Hopefully, you'll persevere even though you may feel exhausted, even though progress is slow, and even though you may have your doubts.

Thankfully, most babies will adopt new sleep habits within a few weeks. But occasionally, an inflexible baby will resist change even though you're doing all the right things. Here are a few strategies that can turn around even the most stubborn donkeys.

The Last Straw: When Nothing Seems to Work

Sometimes a respectful but firm stance is necessary if your baby's sleep habits have deteriorated to the point where no one is getting any sleep. Take Spencer, for example.

Eight-month-old Spencer was a great sleeper until 1 month ago, when he caught his first cold and ended up with an ear infection. Initially, Spencer's ear hurt so much that he was only comfortable snuggled in his mother's arms. After cuddling up next to mom for three glorious nights, Spencer flatly refused to go back in his crib. His mother had no energy to resist, so she said, "Okay, Spencer, you can sleep with Mommy and Daddy." Three weeks later, his mother came to my office. Spencer was still waking up every 2 hours, and his mother fully expected I'd find another ear infection. But I didn't; the problem was purely behavioral.

Every parent I know would rather do a million loads of laundry than allow a baby to "cry it out." However, if you've exhausted the gentle avenues and nothing seems to work, a teeny-tiny bit of crying may be necessary to help your baby get "unstuck."

By 9 months, your baby has probably been nursed or bottle-fed to sleep at least 1,400 times. Suddenly, you decide it's time for a change, and the baby's left hanging: "Have you guys gone mad? How am I supposed to fall asleep?" Babies are not born with a natural ability to fall asleep. Like toilet teaching, it's a skill that must be nurtured and managed.

It's one thing to encourage healthy sleep habits when the WOO is wide open, but it's something entirely different when you try to reverse ineffective sleep habits after they're cemented in stone. Difficult doesn't mean impossible, however.

Earlier in this chapter, we talked about gentle ways to ease your baby into good habits. Sometimes tenacious babies get stuck, and all the gentle kindness in the world doesn't help. They're so darned confused by all the different approaches they've been exposed to that sending a crystal-clear message is the only thing that works. The next two strategies are clear (but kind) messages.

The Gentle Tough Plan

This method is a next-to-last-ditch attempt at nurturing healthy sleep habits with minimal tears.

1. Follow your normal bedtime routine—but don't rock, nurse, or jiggle your baby to sleep. Place her in her crib sleepy-awake.
2. Leave the room and say, "I love you. Now go to sleep."
3. If she cries, hold back a few minutes to see whether she can settle herself. Don't worry that you're inconveniencing your baby; she's developed a sense of permanence and knows you'll return. Plus, she's got all the tools she needs to comfort herself; she just needs encouragement to use them.
4. If she continues crying, step in and offer your support. Do whatever you would normally do to settle your baby down—feeding, rocking, or singing—but eventually she needs to be put back in the crib sleepy-awake.

5. Leave the room and say, "I love you. Now go to sleep." This sends the message "I'm here for you, but nonetheless, I expect you to go to sleep."

6. If your baby starts to cry, repeat the previous steps, but each time you return, spend less time offering comfort. Also, take longer to respond to crying; this is how you encourage your baby to discover self-comforting skills.

7. Go in and out of the room until your baby falls asleep in her crib. Be prepared to do this as long as it takes until she dozes off. I highly recommend you share this job with your partner or other family members—babies have the stamina of Olympic gold medalists.

Notice the difference between this and "Oops, I'll Be Right Back." In the Gentle Tough Plan, you stay *out* of the room and only come in as needed, as opposed to the "Oops" method, where you stay *in* the room and go out for increasing lengths of time. Both approaches send an unequivocal message—"I love you, but it's bedtime"—but the Gentle Tough Plan's message is stronger and more emphatic.

Parents often ask, "How long should we stick with the Gentle Tough Plan before giving up and going on to the next step?" If after a week you're not seeing any signs of improvement (and that's highly unlikely if you're being consistent), then it's time to move on.

The Sleep Fix

This is my least favorite method and certainly not the one I would recommend until you've exhausted all other options.

1. Do the usual bedtime routine, but don't rock, nurse, or jiggle your baby to sleep. Place him in his bed sleepy-awake.

2. Leave the room and say, "I love you. Now go to sleep."
3. If your baby cries, peek in the room to check that he's safe. Say, "I love you. Now go to sleep." Then step out.
4. Keep repeating steps 2 and 3 until your baby dozes off.
5. Repeat the same steps if your baby wakes up during the night.

Now that you understand the significant dangers of sleep deprivation, I hope you understand why I recommend fixing your night owl's sleep habits, even if it involves crying. Crying will not damage your baby's psyche—consider all the love and devotion she's showered with all day. However, sleep deprivation can be lethal.

Common Glitches with Older Babies

My 9-month-old clings to me the moment I get near her crib. I literally need to peel her off before I can get her in.

Because your baby is resisting going into the crib, the first step is to raise her comfort level. Start off by playing together in her bedroom. Don't even acknowledge the crib (but play right next to it). Next, throw toys into the crib, and hold your baby over the side so she can retrieve them. Then put a pile of toys in the crib and let her play there while you remain alongside. The more positive crib memories she collects, the less resistance she'll feel.

> ### WARNING
>
> Please don't leave your baby unattended with a bundle of toys in the crib—this poses a health hazard.

It takes less than 30 seconds for my baby to start crying bloody murder after he realizes he's alone in his crib. What should I do?

Make sure your timing is right, and you're putting him to bed at the first sign of fatigue. A security blanket will also help make this transition a peaceful one. But don't pick him up before giving him a chance to settle unaided.

One night, my 12-month-old was up and down, up and down, for a good 45 minutes before I gave up and brought him into bed with me (where he conked out instantly).

Gentle methods take more time. If possible, have someone lined up to relieve you, like in a relay race. Consistency is crucial; otherwise, your baby learns that it pays to cry and will scream relentlessly until you cave in. Raise your baby's self-calming skills by practicing them during the day. If your baby is fussing, instead of rushing to his aid, say something like "Okay, sweetie, Mommy [or Daddy] will be there in 1 minute," but don't intervene on his behalf until he's had a few moments to settle down. The more your baby practices self-soothing, the faster he'll master this skill.

My baby nods off without too much trouble but is wide awake and raring to go 10 to 20 minutes later. What's going on?

Most likely, your baby is having trouble falling into a deep sleep. The best way to deal with this is to beat her to the punch. Ten minutes after you put her down, hum and say "shush" until she's transitioned into a deep sleep.

I've been using the H.E.L.P. strategy for 2 weeks now without results. Why isn't it working?

Two weeks is an awfully long time to be trying without results. Most likely your timing needs to be adjusted; your baby is either overtired or too awake when you put him down. Don't put your baby to bed according to the clock but, rather, begin the bedtime routine when your baby shows the first signs of fatigue.

The instant I put 9-month-old Sarah to bed, she pulls herself up, rattles the handrails, and cries bitterly.

Sarah sounds angry more than anything. Let her vent for a few minutes. Some babies get bored with venting and start to play, while others get more and more worked up and need your H.E.L.P. to settle down. Begin with the "Oops, I'll Be Right Back" strategy; if after 1 week your baby is not sleeping better, go to the next level of encouragement: the Gentle Tough Plan. Give your baby a week to improve her sleep skills, and if she doesn't (which is rare), she needs the Sleep Fix.

As soon as I pop my 8-month-old in the crib, he alternates between fussing and playing. This can go on for a good half hour before he gets angry and loses it. Should I put him to bed later?

Don't put your baby to bed later—that half hour provides great self-calming practice. With your H.E.L.P, about 80 percent of older babies will sleep soundly within 7 days of starting the Lull-a-Baby Sleep Plan.

THE RULE OF 9'S

Last year, I carried out an informal study in my office to see if a window of opportunity existed to *fix* sleep problems. I found that it was much easier to establish healthy sleep habits during the WOO, which is from approximately 2 to 7 months of age. It's easier to *fix* sleep problems from 7 to 9 months of age. After that time, there's more crying involved and it takes longer to see results—but it's still possible.

What if my baby stands up in the crib and won't settle down? She's as happy as a clam but won't go to sleep.

As long as your baby is entertaining herself, there's no need to intervene. Eventually, she'll wind down and go to sleep.

CHEAT SHEET: TOP SEVEN TIPS FOR SOLVING BIG-KID SLEEP PROBLEMS

1. **Allow a little frustration to serve as motivation for change.** You don't need to let your baby cry herself silly, but there's nothing wrong with a bit of frustration.

2. **Believe in your baby's ability to change.** Trust his ability to grow and learn.

3. **Create the "right" backdrop.** Choose bedtime conditions that encourage sleep.

4. **Choose a happy ending (and beginning and middle).** You are more likely to stick with a program if you feel good about the process.

5. **H.E.L.P. your baby fall asleep.** Hang back, Empathize, Love, and Persevere to gently sleep-train an older baby.

6. **"Oops, I'll Be Right Back!"** Step out of the room, taking increasingly longer times to return, and your baby will eventually find her own way to the Land of Nod.

7. **Fade out.** Become less involved as time goes by, until you fade right out of the picture.

Fade Away

I ended the book with this chapter because I wanted to give you a Hollywood ending. I picked this particular phrase because I want you to remember to fade out—to become less involved—as your baby's healthy sleep habits kick in. This means that as your baby becomes more adept at falling asleep, you wean yourself out of whatever support you've provided.

For instance, if you've been using the "Oops, I'll Be Right Back" routine, take longer and longer periods of time to return to the room, until your baby is no longer fussing when you leave and falls asleep before you return.

Now that your baby is going to bed without a fuss and sleeping for longer periods, it's your turn to look after yourself. "Me-time" is not a dirty word. There will always be housework to do and errands to run. But if your personal time comes at the bottom of the to-do list, you'll never get to it. Even if you carve out only 10 minutes for yourself, enjoy it, because inside every mother is a person who could use a little nurturing herself.

$\mathscr{K}$EEP IN TOUCH!

Before we part ways, I want to congratulate you on unselfishly accepting less sleep when you probably needed it most. I bet there were times when you felt like giving up—but like a true hero, you carried on. And now, all your love and devotion is paying off! Not only is your baby sleeping through the night but she's babbling, flirting, and learning how to grab the heart of everyone who meets her. As a direct consequence of his new sleep habits, your baby is more sociable, curious, and engaging, and his personality sparkles like diamonds. I hope you feel proud of your accomplishment!

Before we part ways, let me say, I hope my advice helped you find your way to the Land of Nod, and that I was able to make this journey less exhausting and stressful and more loving and calm. If you ever feel that sleep problems are just too darn big to tackle or you have some doubts about whether your baby is capable of changing, you can find support and motivation online at www.mylullababy. com. I sincerely hope you'll get in touch with me if you encounter problems or have questions not covered in this book!

Finally, it's time to say good night and turn out the lights . . .

—*Dr. C.*

ANSWERS TO ALL YOUR A TO Z-Z-Z QUESTIONS

ADOPTION

Although your beautiful new baby is sure to be showered with love and attention, initially, no effort should be made to adjust his sleep habits; he has enough changes to contend with. Gather as much information, in as much detail as possible, about your baby's bedtime routine, and stick with what he already knows. On the other hand, if your baby already has super falling-asleep skills, make sure you don't do anything to jeopardize them—even if you find it unbearable to be apart.

APNEA

Apnea is a Greek word that means "without wind." Apnea is an abnormal pause in breathing that lasts 20 seconds or more and should be distinguished from periodic breathing (see BREATHING NOISES), which is an innocent pause in a newborn's breathing pattern during sleep. Apnea can be a problem if pauses last longer than 20 seconds. If you suspect your child has apnea, please consult your doctor.

APNEA MONITOR

Baby apnea monitors are devices that are intended to prevent SIDS or other life-threatening events by sounding a loud alarm when a baby's breathing slows or stops. The simplest models can be bought in department stores and online. Unfortunately, there is no literature or solid scientific studies to support their "lifesaving" value. If you're thinking, "If it potentially protects my baby, I don't care about lack of evidence," you need to know about the downside of these monitors. False alarms may occur when a baby moves or breathes shallowly or if the leads become loose. This causes enormous stress and sometimes even unnecessary interventions. I suggest you rely instead on scientifically proven SIDS-prevention practices, including back sleeping, safe sleeping environments, and elimination of secondhand smoke. If your baby has a medical condition that requires home apnea monitoring, your doctor will give you guidelines for the proper equipment.

BABY BLUES

Up to 40 percent of new moms are plagued by unhappy feelings mixed with joy during the first few weeks as a new mom. Women suffer from three degrees of depression—the baby blues, postpartum depression, and postpartum psychosis. The baby blues are most common; anyone who's given birth is familiar with the incredible range of emotions. You may feel elated but terrified, exhausted but exhilarated, tearful but joyful—a virtual baby-basketful of conflicting emotions. Some women experience a deeper degree of sadness, confusion, anxiety, fear, loneliness, and insomnia. Thankfully, true postpartum psychosis—which includes bizarre behavior, paranoia, and hallucinations—is extremely rare.

If you (or someone you know) is suffering from postpartum depression, please realize you are not alone, and seek medical attention. In addition, support is available through:

- Postpartum Support International: 805-967-7636 or www. postpartum.net. This site has a self-quiz that helps you identify and understand your feelings.
- *Down Came the Rain: My Journey through Postpartum Depression,* by Brooke Shields (Hyperion, May 2005). In this book, the model/actress describes her own struggle with the condition.

BABYSITTER

Sadly, 20 percent of SIDS occurs with secondary caregivers. A baby who generally sleeps in the back-to-sleep position but is put on the tummy by a sitter or at daycare has 18 to 20 times the risk for SIDS. All caregivers must be made aware of the necessity of the back-to-sleep position.

BACK TO SLEEP

One of the most successful ways to reduce the risk of SIDS is to put your baby in bed on his back, even for naps. Since the introduction of the back-to-sleep position, the annual incidence of SIDS has been reduced by 50 percent. Everyone—daycare workers, grandparents, babysitters, uncles, aunts, and girlfriends—should understand that a baby must always be put down to sleep on his back. Once a baby can turn from back to tummy and tummy to back, he should continue to be put in the crib on his back but allowed to sleep in the position of his choice. Many parents worry that their baby will choke if he spits up or vomits, but studies show that the back-to-sleep position does not cause an increase in choking or aspiration.

BALD SPOT

The back-to-sleep position may cause a temporary bald spot at the back of a baby's head. This will lessen as a baby begins to sit up and will disappear completely when more hair grows.

BASSINET

Many parents keep a bassinet close to their bed for the first few months to keep their baby within arm's reach all night long. However, babies outgrow bassinets quickly; by the end of the first month, or when your baby weighs about 10 pounds, stop using a bassinet. All safety guidelines for cribs also apply to bassinets. Log on to the Consumer Product Safety Commission's Web site at www.cpsc.gov to check for recalls before purchasing a bassinet.

BED SHARING

Rather than argue its merits, let's focus on safety issues. Here are 10 ways to bed-share safely.

- Never allow your baby to sleep on a water bed.
- Consider using a cosleeper attachment.
- Don't fall asleep on the couch with your baby next to you.
- Keep your baby swaddled all night long.
- Eliminate any space between the mattress and the wall or headboard.
- Do not use pillows, comforters, or loose bedding that could smother your baby.
- Use the back-to-sleep position, even if you're right next to your baby.
- Don't bed-share if you're on medication that makes you sleepy or if you've consumed alcohol.
- Be aware that one of the biggest risks of bed sharing appears to

occur when a baby sleeps with someone other than parents (including other children).

- Don't put your baby to bed near curtains or blinds that have a dangling draw cord.

BOTTLES

While I unconditionally support breastfeeding, I recognize that giving the occasional bottle isn't a tragedy.

BREASTFEEDING OR BOTTLE-FEEDING TO SLEEP

Mother Nature intended tiny babies to fall asleep by suckling. Unfortunately, she neglected to mention that this habit should be discontinued around 2 to 4 months of age.

BREATHING NOISES

GROANS AND MOANS: Some babies naturally grunt and groan as they move about in their sleep.

PERIODIC BREATHING: Newborns have periods of panting that last 10 to 15 seconds, followed by a brief pause that lasts just a few seconds—although it seems like forever—and then normal breathing starts again.

SQUEAKY SOUNDS: Some babies make a high-pitched crowing sound, like a pennywhistle, when breathing in because their airways are floppy. This disappears by the first birthday.

STUFFY NOISES: A newborn naturally breathes through the nose during sleep. Consequently, she breathes in dust, molds, and other environmental irritants, which may cause her nasal passages to swell and sound stuffed up. I tell parents that they can distinguish a cold from a stuffy nose by whether a baby's nose is running—if it's not, she doesn't have a cold.

BRIEF AWAKENINGS

Sleep has light and deep stages. During a light sleep state, which occurs every few hours, it's normal for babies to briefly awaken, shuffle, and make squeaky noises, but with the Lull-a-Baby Sleep Plan, they learn to relax and fall back to sleep. (Every single book about infant sleep habits assumes that a baby has formed unhealthy sleep associations. Hopefully, you took advantage of the WOO, and healthy sleep memories were formed when it counted, so babies know exactly what to do when they awaken briefly.)

BUMPER PADS

Using bumper pads is no longer recommended because they represent a substantial entanglement, entrapment, strangulation, and suffocation hazard. Bumper pads restrict the flow of oxygen-rich air around the infant, which poses a higher risk of SIDS. Other hazards associated with bumper pads:

- Ribbons used to secure the pads to the slats can cause suffocation or entanglement.
- A mobile baby might use bumper pads for climbing and fall out of the crib.
- Loose stitching can become tangled around fingers and toes.
- Bumper pads that do not fit perfectly can cause suffocation.

CAFFEINE

While most nursing babies aren't stimulated by Mom's coffee, a touchy baby may get revved up and find it difficult to unwind. You don't need to avoid coffee all day; just don't make it an evening ritual.

CAR SEATS

After spending 9 months cuddly-squished in the womb, young babies often sleep best all curled up. While sleeping in a car seat may look scrunchy-uncomfortable, babies prefer a snug fit. Many parents ask me, "Will sleeping in the car seat hurt my baby's spine or cause a crick in the neck?" While the answer is no, your baby, nonetheless, is better off in a crib. A baby who sleeps well in a car seat tends to sleep best swaddled as snug as a bug in a rug.

CIRCADIAN RHYTHM

Our sleep is governed by biological cycles that repeat about every 24 hours. Interestingly, a baby's biological clock begins to operate around 6 weeks of age—just as the WOO is cracking open!

COLDS

A baby with a cold may feel lousy and sleep poorly. A cold is tough on a baby because she can't breathe through her nose or blow it yet. Realistically, you should expect a baby who isn't feeling well to relapse in her sleep habits.

See Your Doctor If . . .	
Newborn to 4 Months of Age	**4 Months to 1 Year of Age**
Fever is present.	Fever is present more than 48 hours.
Your baby is coughing, choking, or vomiting.	Your baby is coughing, choking, or vomiting.
Your baby is not feeding well or has fewer wet diapers than usual.	Your baby isn't drinking or eating well or has fewer wet diapers than usual.
Your baby is irritable, shows a decreased activity level, or is not making eye contact.	Your baby is fussy even when held, seems lethargic, or won't stop crying.
Symptoms persist more than a few days or worsen.	Cold symptoms persist more than a week or are getting worse instead of better.
Breathing is shallow, rapid, or labored, or you hear wheezing or other high-pitched or whistling noises.	Breathing is rapid or labored, or you hear wheezing or high-pitched whistling noises.
You feel concerned.	You feel concerned.

As you know, there is no cure for the common cold—but there are ways to increase your baby's comfort level. Here are eight home remedies that will help your baby sleep better.

1. ELEVATE THE HEAD OF THE BED. Your baby's nasal passages will be less clogged if you take advantage of gravity. Do not use a pillow in the crib; instead, place a small one under the mattress as long as the fit remains snug and there is less than two-fingers' width between mattress and frame.

2. USE A NASAL ASPIRATOR. Since a baby can't blow his nose, loosen secretions with saline nose drops, and then remove the mucus using a nasal bulb, or nasal aspirator. He'll feel better and sleep for longer stretches when he's not all stuffed up. (To use a nasal aspirator, squeeze air out of the bulb, insert the tip gently into a nostril, then release the bulb slowly; repeat if needed. Be careful—overuse of a bulb syringe can irritate the lining of a child's nose.)

3. FEED CHICKEN SOUP. If your baby is old enough, offer chicken soup. Research suggests that chicken soup has anti-inflammatory properties that inhibit mucus-stimulating substances. Plus, there's something magical that science can't explain about the healing properties of chicken soup.

4. BE SELECTIVE ABOUT MEDICINE. Here is a review of over-the-counter cold preparations.

   • COLD REMEDIES
   Cold remedies contain a combination of antihistamines and decongestants, which may have side effects such as hyperactivity, sleeplessness, and irritability. I do not recommend these products for babies.

- COUGH SYRUPS

  Coughing is beneficial because it clears the lungs; therefore, it is not wise to suppress it with cough medicine. You can best relieve a stubborn cough by humidifying the air in your child's bedroom to loosen mucus. (Clean the humidifier daily to prevent mold and bacteria buildup.)

- DECONGESTANTS

  I do not recommend these for babies. Decongestants dry up a stuffy nose and make breathing easier, but they have a number of unpleasant side effects. Babies taking these medications may act hyper, feel anxious, have a racing heart, or find it difficult to sleep.

- NOSE DROPS (DECONGESTANT)

  A nasal decongestant should never be given to an infant because too much of the medication can be absorbed through the nasal membranes.

- NOSE DROPS (SALTWATER/SALINE)

  If your baby is sleeping and feeding well, there is no need to mess with the nose. But if sleep or feeding is a problem, saltwater nose drops can help. Put a drop or two into a nostril at a time, then aspirate so your baby can breathe easier.

5. USE A COOL-MIST HUMIDIFIER. Humid air makes mucus more slippery, which is why running a humidifier in your baby's room can help. (Make sure to change the water daily to prevent mold!) Alternatively, you can go into the bathroom, close the door, and turn on a hot shower. Allow your baby to breathe in the steam for two 10-minute sessions a day.

6. ICKY RAW-NOSE RELIEF. A comfortable baby will sleep better. You can prevent a red, raw nose by applying a thick layer of
   petroleum jelly to the skin under the nose. Also, wipe your
   baby's nose with an extrasoft tissue or cloth diaper.

7. HUGS. Nothing works better than a parent's hug when a baby
   is under the weather. Often, parents worry that a baby who
   cries whenever he's placed in the crib has an ear infection, but
   more often than not, it's just that your baby feels best when
   cuddled in your arms.

8. SMALL, FREQUENT FEEDINGS. A young baby may not be
   able to nurse and breathe at the same time, so shorter but more
   frequent feedings are beneficial. A baby who's already eating
   solids can eat any food she likes, but don't be surprised if she
   doesn't have much interest in eating. (*Note:* Contrary to folk
   wisdom, you don't need to avoid milk when your baby has a
   cold. This belief has been studied scientifically, and milk hasn't
   been found to increase mucus production.)

COLIC

Some babies are so discombobulated by their new world that they
can't settle down. About 5 percent of babies need loud white noise,
constant motion, and cuddles to help them sleep. It can be very
frustrating and physically exhausting for the parents of a "colicky"
baby. It may take up to 3 months for a frazzled baby to adjust
to the rhythm, feel, and sensations of the world around him. In
the meantime, you can help your baby sleep using the following
strategies.

- Contrary to what your intuition may tell you, some young
  infants need noise to help them sleep. Turn on the static
  between radio stations, and leave it playing loud—dishwashers,

vacuum cleaners, and white-noise machines are also great sources of white noise. (I recently discovered The First Years Nature's Lullaby Player, a voice-activated device that turns on when a baby cries and plays either preprogrammed nature sounds or lullabies.)

- Instead of taking your baby for a car ride, put him in a swinging chair. Parents often worry this will lead to a dependency— but it won't. It will, however, tide you over until your baby adapts to life outside the womb. (See SWINGING CHAIRS for safety considerations.)
- Swaddling gives a baby the same sense of nestling she experienced in the womb. Turn to page 88 for directions on how to swaddle so your baby feels lovingly embraced.

CRIB SAFETY

New cribs almost certainly conform to safety standards. To be sure your crib is safe, keep in mind these tips.

- If you've inherited a crib from a family member or a friend, make certain your baby's crib meets all federal safety regulations. For more information, contact the Consumer Product Safety Commission at 800-638-2772 or log on to www.cpsc.gov.
- The mattress should fit tightly, without any gaps between it and the sides of the crib.
- Crib sheets should fit snugly.
- Do not use a plastic mattress cover.
- Remove decorative ribbons, ties, bumper pads, and bows.
- Don't hang objects that a baby can pull down.
- Do not use a pillow in the crib.
- Do not use sleep aids to keep your baby positioned in the crib.

- Inspect the crib for missing or broken hardware.
- Check to see that all slats are no more than $2^3/_8$ inches apart.
- Corner posts should not be over $^1/_{16}$ inch high.
- Headboards and footboards should not have cutout designs.
- A safety-certification seal should be present on a new crib.

CRYING

A newborn can't tell you why he's crying because he doesn't know himself. He just knows he's unhappy. During the first few months of life, until the WOO opens, it's difficult to interpret one cry from another. Please don't feel frustrated if you can't initially understand your baby's cry. Researchers in Finland found that when baby nurses were asked to listen to recorded sounds of hungry, uncomfortable, and delighted babies, they were able to correctly identify *why* a baby was crying only *50 percent* of the time. If the pros aren't perfect baby readers, how can you expect yourself to be? Around 3 months of age, when a baby comes out of his shell, he'll use different cries to mean different things—and, thank goodness, he'll be easier to read. (One of the most bizarre products on the market is a baby-cry analyzer, a device that indicates the reason a baby is crying. Save your money and trust your instincts.)

DAY/NIGHT CONFUSION

Babies aren't born with a sense of day and night; they sleep and eat in bits and pieces around the clock. Sometimes a baby seems to be asleep all day and awake all night. Studies have shown that day/night confusion can be reversed quickly when parents exaggerate the difference between the two. For example, when you feed your baby during the day, talk to her using a perky singsong voice, stroke her hair, and keep the room bright. At night, whisper or talk; just feed your baby and pop her back in bed. Keep the light dim and the room dark, and breathe deeply and slowly (to pass on a mellow mood).

DEHYDRATION

Although you will hear "Never wake a sleeping baby," the first 48 hours of a baby's life is the exception to the rule. Babies lose body water in the first few days of life and can become dehydrated quickly. Newborns need to feed frequently and should be woken if sleeping for extended periods. Your physician will advise you how often your baby needs to feed, depending on birth weight, weight loss, and overall health.

DIAPERS

Until a month of age, a baby has a gastro-colic reflex, which means he poops each time he feeds. But after this time, he'll have fewer poopy diapers, and you won't need to routinely change him during the night. Use a superabsorbent diaper and a thick barrier cream—and enjoy more sleep.

EARACHE

When a parent thinks a baby is sleeping poorly due to an ear infection, I ask, "Is your baby happy during the daytime?" If the answer is yes, then I know an ear infection likely isn't the root of the problem. You can't turn ear pain on and off; either it's there or it's not. Yes, it's worse when lying down, but it won't be absent at other times. If you're unsure, however, have your health care provider take a peek.

EARLY AWAKENING

Sometimes you can eke out extra shut-eye by encouraging your baby to play quietly in his crib when he wakes up in the morning. This will happen naturally if you postpone going into the baby's room for early risings. Many parents try keeping a baby up later hoping he'll sleep in, but this rarely works; a baby's brain registers morning noises (cars driving by, birds chirping) even while sleeping. One way around this is to play white noise all night and keep the room darkened.

EYES ROLLING BACK

As a newborn falls asleep, her eyes may roll back, or she may even sleep with her eyes open because the eye muscles are undeveloped and relatively weak.

FEVER

A baby who has a fever needs extra fluids, cuddles, and comfort. You may need to feed your baby every few hours during the night, especially if he hasn't fed well during the day. Naturally, your baby's comfort and well-being are the main priorities until he's well. (Please discuss fever management with your physician, so you know how to respond and when to seek medical advice and help.)

FLAT HEAD

Although putting a baby to sleep on his back may help prevent SIDS, many babies develop a flat head. This does not cause brain damage but does affect his appearance. Flattening of the skull can be avoided by changing a baby's position often throughout the day. Encourage tummy time when your baby is awake, and put your baby to bed at opposite ends of the crib each week. Keep one side of the crib interesting and the other side boring to encourage your baby to turn his head from side to side.

FORMULA

Sometimes a mother who is breastfeeding asks me, "Will my baby sleep longer if I give formula at bedtime?" By 6 months of age (or earlier), most babies wake up because they lack falling-asleep skills, not because of hunger. So, no, unfortunately, a bedtime bottle or something like it won't lengthen sleep time.

FUSSY BABIES

A fussy baby will have less predictable sleep and feeding habits and therefore be more challenging to put to bed. If your baby has no set bedtime or naptimes, watch her closely for a week, and note when she shows the first signs of fatigue. Remember, increased fussiness, decreased coordination, droopy eyes, yawning, and endless or more vigorous suckling all suggest tiredness. Record those signs, and a pattern will reveal itself.

GADGETS, GIZMOS, AND GIMMICKS

It's been said that it takes a village to raise a child, but it appears to take a warehouse full of gadgets to equip a baby. Is all this stuff *really* necessary? Before you take out a second mortgage, let's take a critical look at what helps, what doesn't come close, and what might even work against you.

- BABY MONITOR: Baby monitors offer peace of mind. Plus, some of these gadgets offer walkie-talkie features, which means you can sh-sh-sh your baby without going in. And that's not all—you can even remotely activate a mattress vibrator.

  Interestingly, no reliable studies have been done to evaluate whether all the bells and whistles make a difference, so I asked the parents in my practice to share their experiences. Here is a sampling of the most common responses.

  Marla: "I can't imagine life without a monitor. I like to know what's going on behind my back."

  Jeff: "I sleep better hearing my son's every breath. We have the walkie-talkie kind of monitor, but we rarely use that feature. We feel it would be like teasing him—he can hear us, but he can't see us."

  Vicki: "I'm a little anxious at the best of times, so I bought a monitor that would allow me to see and hear my baby. I thought it would be nice to be able to talk to my little guy from my bedroom. My son loves the vibrating mattress and will often settle without me—if I use it before he has any serious complaints."

Lee: "I love being able to hear my little princess, and she loves being able to hear me."

Bryce: "Whenever I used the vibrating mattress, my son cried, so I stopped."

Obviously, every baby is different, and it's impossible to predict whether a certain feature will be a benefit or not.

- BATTERY-OPERATED SWINGING CHAIR: Newborns need motion like mothers need sleep. A swing is the perfect way to help a baby relax before bedtime.
- BOUNCY SEAT: Since most of us don't have endless villagers to share baby care, it's helpful to have somewhere to put a baby down from time to time. Please remember, however, that a bouncy chair is not a bed.
- CRIB BLOX: These tiny feet raise the head of the bed about 2 inches. When a baby has a runny nose, raising the head of the bed prevents secretions from pooling in the throat. A 2-inch elevation, however, isn't much help.
- CRIB MOBILE: Considering that a newborn can't see more than 9 to 12 inches, a mobile provides relief in an otherwise fuzzy world. This focal point calms a baby and allows him to drift off. Remember, however, mobiles should be removed when a baby is able to reach toward objects. Another word of caution: Don't use the mobile's music box to help your baby fall asleep, as this will become a habit that later needs to be broken.
- DIMMER: Anything that helps a baby learn the difference

between day and night is a good thing. Dimmers on lights will allow you to see during the night without giving your baby the impression that it's time to get up.

- ROCKING CRADLE: Battery-operated rocking cradles and models that use a spring for a more natural movement soothe tiny babies to sleep, especially during the first months of life, when a baby craves her womb-room. Once the WOO opens, these items should be used for relaxing but not for sleeping. See www.ambybaby.com for motion-activated cradles.
- SIDE BED: A cosleeper is a side bed that snuggles up next to Mom and Dad's bed. In fact, it's better than cosleeping: You get all the advantages without any risks. For those who want to go the family-bed route, a cosleeper is a brilliant product.
- SLEEP POSITIONER: The safety of these items has not been tested. I do not recommend them.
- SWADDLING BLANKET: Babies sleep better and longer when swaddled. If you have difficulty managing a swaddle on your own, consider one of these blankets. They simplify the folding process enormously.
- ZIP-AROUND SAFETY BLANKET: Cute, but are they necessary? Only if they give you peace of mind.

GAS

Is your baby waking up during the night because of gas pains? There are basically three situations that result in excessive gas: (1) swallowing air while feeding or crying; (2) digestive problems (lactose intolerance or milk protein allergy); or (3) a natural by-product of digestion. Realistically, most babies wake up because of insufficient sleep skills as opposed to excessive gas. Here are three key questions I ask parents to determine whether gas is causing sleep problems.

*Does your baby appear to have gas pains during the day?

If not, then it's unlikely your baby is waking up because of excessive gas.

* Does your baby settle down when held?

If yes, then it's unlikely your baby is suffering from excessive gas.

* Do antigas medications eliminate the problem?

If yes, then it's likely your baby is suffering from excessive gas.

What sometimes confuses people is that all babies look as if they're in pain when they're wailing. They pump their little legs, arch their backs, and turn red in the face. Gas is a problem of tiny babies that resolves on its own, typically by 2 months of age. Although gas may not be waking your baby up, here are a few strategies to ease his tummy.

- BURPING UPGRADE. Try different burping strategies. My favorite burping hold is what I call a chin-up. Hold your baby upright, facing away from you, and cup her chin in your hand. Pat her back, up and down, until a burp surfaces.
- SLOW DOWN FEEDINGS. Taking breaks during feedings to burp your baby reduces gas.
- GAS DROPS. Studies show that over-the-counter gas drops are not effective; however, many parents swear by them.

RED FLAGS: SEE YOUR DOCTOR IF YOUR BABY HAS GAS WITH:

- Loose, foul stools
- Poor weight gain
- Vomiting
- Irritability
- Sleep problems accompanied by the above

HAND-ME-DOWNS

To verify safety of secondhand purchases and hand-me-downs, check out www.recalls.gov or www.cpsc.gov.

HEAD BANGING

Although parents worry that something must be emotionally or intellectually "wrong" with a baby who bangs his head, believe it or not, the rhythmic movement soothes an infant. Bonking his head repeatedly against the headboard or rails may help him fall asleep; it won't harm your baby's developing brain or cause a headache, so there is no reason to discourage head banging. The baby who bangs his head to fall asleep will typically outgrow the behavior between 18 and 30 months of age. (However, if your baby bangs his head out of frustration or has developmental delays, a chat with your health care provider is needed.) If you absolutely hate head banging, try this trick from one of my patients: "Eight-month-old Maggie would bang her head on the headboard for a solid 20 minutes before dozing off. One morning, I found a bruise on her forehead and decided this had gone too far. So, I put a metronome in her room and set it to match the rate at which she bangs her head. Although she didn't entirely stop head banging, she cut down significantly. Hallelujah!"

HOSPITALIZATION

Setbacks in sleep habits are inevitable after a hospitalization. Give yourself and your baby some time to recover before working on sleep habits, but think carefully about how you handle sleep in the interim. The more ineffective habits you allow to develop, the bigger the adjustment when sleep training resumes.

ILLNESS (See also COLDS)

An infant who is ill or has a fever needs extra fluids, so encourage him to drink, day and night. Once your baby is better, work on sleep habits without delay. Many parents make the mistake of thinking, "My baby used to sleep through the night, so if I wait long enough, he'll do it again." Remember, your baby needs you to provide direction, not the other way around.

IMMUNIZATIONS

The Institute of Medicine investigated whether immunizations increase the risk of SIDS and concluded that there is no evidence linking vaccines with SIDS, sudden unexpected death in infancy, or neonatal death. On the other hand, immunizations may cause a baby to be cranky, feverish, and generally out of sorts for 24 to 48 hours. Comforting your baby should be your number one priority during this time, but get back on track as soon as possible.

JEWELRY

Many traditional customs involve babies wearing trinkets, such as a bracelet or necklace believed to protect against the evil eye. Although I am a great believer in the value of tradition, a baby should not be put to bed with anything tied around the neck or attached by a string.

LACTOSE INTOLERANCE

If a baby wakes up howling, many parents assume gas caused by lactose intolerance is the problem. Lactose intolerance implies an inability to digest lactose, the sugar found in cow's milk, breast milk, and dairy products. An individual with lactose intolerance lacks enough of the lactase enzyme needed to digest lactose. The undigested lactose sits in the gut and causes gas, a distended abdomen, stomach cramps, diarrhea, and irritability. The good news is that true lactose intolerance is extremely rare during infancy. However, some babies suffer from a functional lactose intolerance—the lactase enzyme is present but not working up to par. This is a temporary problem that resolves on its own within a few months. Formula-fed babies with either a true or functional lactose intolerance will benefit from a lactose-free formula, while a breastfed baby with lactose intolerance should be encouraged to empty one breast before being offered the other to ensure they're getting the high-fat hind milk. This is because the composition of breast milk changes during feeds. First is the foremilk, which is like skim milk (low in fat and calories). As the feeding continues, the fat content increases, resembling whole milk. The end of the feed is like a yummy dessert, high in fat and calories. The hindmilk, with its high fat content, slows down the speed of the tummy emptying. Slower is better because the tummy has less lactose to digest at any one time.

RED FLAGS: SEE YOUR DOCTOR IF YOUR BABY:

- Has gas and bloating 24-7
- Is vomiting and spitting up (not associated with burps or jiggling)
- Seems irritable, especially if worse about a half hour after feeds
- Has watery, explosive stools
- Has sleep problems accompanied by the above

LOVEYS

Transitional objects help make bedtime less lonely and more relaxing. A lovey should not be left in the crib, however, until a baby is rolling over. Make sure the object is safe. Stuffed animals should not have any ties, ribbons, eyes, or other parts that are stitched or glued on (no matter how secure they appear); they may pose a choking hazard. Look for sturdy construction at the seams. Avoid toys stuffed with pellets, which pose a choking danger. Luckily, you can find plenty of stuffed animals that are safe.

MASSAGE

Although it is hard to find reliable studies on massage and its effect on sleep, current literature suggests that babies who are massaged for 15 minutes before bedtime have fewer sleep problems. (See page 54 for step-by-step instructions, and then give your baby one tonight.)

MILK ALLERGY

Many parents suspect that a baby who doesn't sleep well suffers from a food allergy. Up to 7 percent of babies suffer from an allergy to the protein in cow's milk and cow's milk–based formulas. This means the immune system attacks that protein, and an allergic reaction follows, either immediately or with a delayed onset. An immediate allergic reaction occurs suddenly and includes wheezing, vomiting, hives, and/or total collapse (anaphylaxis). A more common allergic reaction is one with a slower onset and more subtle signs, such as loose stools (blood may be present), irritability, gas, and failure to gain weight. (However, irritability alone is not diagnostic of a milk allergy!) A baby with a sudden-onset food allergy is easier to diagnose because the symptoms appear immediately after feeding; a slow-onset food allergy is more subtle and may be confused with other health problems. A baby diagnosed with a milk protein allergy will be switched to a soy-based or hypoallergenic formula, and the symptoms will resolve entirely. (Bear in mind that 8 to 15 percent of people allergic to milk are also allergic to soy.) Many babies outgrow a slow-onset milk allergy by age 2.

RED FLAGS: SEE YOUR DOCTOR IF YOUR BABY HAS:

- Hives or vomiting after feeding
- Inadequate weight gain
- Blood in stools
- Irritability and excessive gas
- Poor sleep in combination with the above

MISCONCEPTIONS

Parents often assume a medical condition explains a change in a baby's sleep habits. Here are some common health misconceptions.

- "IF A BABY CRIES WHEN YOU PUT HIM DOWN, HE PROBABLY HAS AN EAR INFECTION." In my experience, if a baby is then perfectly happy when picked up, ear pain isn't the issue.
- "IF A BABY PULLS AT HER EARS, THEY MUST HURT." A happy baby who doesn't have a history of ear infections is more likely to be teething or exploring her ears than suffering from an infection.
- "A GASSY BABY NEEDS A CHANGE IN FORMULA." If a baby is happy and gaining weight well, there's no reason to switch. Swallowed air happens regardless of what kind of formula is used. However, it's worth considering a change to a feeding system designed to prevent babies from swallowing air.
- "IF MY BABY SNORES, HIS ADENOIDS MUST BE ENLARGED." Young babies prefer to breathe through the nose, especially at night. Their tiny nasal passages become inflamed, which causes heavy breathing that sounds a lot like snoring. Adenoids don't typically cause problems in the first year of life; they're too small to begin with.
- "MY BABY MUST BE IN PAIN OR HUNGRY; OTHERWISE, SHE WOULDN'T WAKE UP FROM SLEEP." I'm sure you now know that babies wake up because of brief night awakenings but may cry out because they lack falling-asleep skills.
- "MY BABY GNAWS ON EVERYTHING IN SIGHT, SO HE MUST BE TEETHING." Nine times out of 10, teething is not

the issue: A baby begins to explore his environment by putting everything, including his fist, in his mouth. (See TEETHING for more information.)

MOBILE

Tiny babies love crib mobiles. Those sold in stores should meet safety standards that limit string length (no longer than 7 inches) and reduce the risk of strangulation. However, beware of old mobiles, those not intended for cribs, and homemade ones. For safety reasons, a mobile should be removed before a baby is sitting. Better yet, remove mobiles once the WOO appears so your baby doesn't become dependent on it.

MOVING

Babies are more perceptive than we think. Therefore, an effort should be made to minimize the stress of moving. The best way to do this is to keep the crib decor the same and resume sleep rituals as soon as possible. If sleep has been challenging, I'd go so far as keeping the north/south orientation of the crib the same, too!

NEWBORN

When is a newborn no longer a newborn? Look up *newborn* in a dictionary, and the most common definition is "a baby recently born, usually less than 1 month of age." While accurate, this superficial description doesn't adequately describe the phenomenally fast developments that occur in the first few weeks of life that separate a newborn from a baby. And as the newborn stage comes to a close, the WOO opens.

NIGHT-LIGHTS

Night-lights appear to be safe. A study reported in the *British Journal of Ophthalmology* found no difference in myopia (nearsightedness) between night-light users and nonusers.

NIGHTMARES

No one really knows whether babies have nightmares because they can't tell us, but scientists suspect they do. As a parent, I'd have to agree. I remember many a night when one of my kids woke up crying like I'd never heard before. It's hard to recognize a nightmare before your baby is sleeping through the night because there is already plenty of fussing and crying. But when a good sleeper wakes up wailing for no apparent reason, I prefer to err on the side of safety and assume something is wrong. A nightmare is one consideration. Clearly, it's best to pick your baby up and comfort her if you think she's had a bad dream.

OBSTACLES

Lots of ideas look great on paper, but when you try to implement them, the realities of day-to-day life interfere. For instance, it's hard to put your baby down for a nap if it's time to get your older child from daycare. It's hard to spend the extra time charming a baby to sleep when you've brought home tons of work from the office that's due the next day. Modern life is packed with complications, but don't let the obstacles of daily life discourage you from trying your best.

PACIFIER

If you choose to give your baby a pacifier, the following considerations will help you do so safely.

- Choose a one-piece model; some can break into two pieces.
- The shield should have air holes, be made of firm plastic, and be big enough so that the whole pacifier will not fit in the baby's mouth.
- Select the size appropriate for your baby.
- Try different nipple shapes until you discover the one your

baby prefers. (There is no definitive evidence that orthodontic nipples are best.)

- Choose a dishwasher-safe pacifier.
- Wash pacifiers before using them the first time and regularly thereafter, following the manufacturer's instructions.
- Never, ever tie a pacifier around your baby's neck or hand or attach one to the crib because of the risk of strangulation.
- Do not use the nipple from a baby bottle as a pacifier; if a baby sucks hard enough, the nipple can pop out and pose a choking hazard.
- Replace a pacifier when the nipple has changed color or is torn.
- Do not clean a pacifier by popping it in your mouth.

PETS

Pets may experience "sibling" rivalry when a new baby arrives on the scene. No pet, no matter how docile or gentle, should be allowed in the nursery when your baby is asleep or allowed into the crib, play-pen, swinging chair, or car seat.

PILLOWS

Infants should not sleep with a pillow, even a small flat one, and not even to elevate the head of a baby with a cold. A cosleeping infant should be kept away from pillows, blankets, and comforters.

POSITIONAL DEVICES

These devices should not be used. The only position an infant should be put to sleep in is flat on the back.

PREMATURE BABIES

A premature baby should not be encouraged to sleep through the night until you get the okay from your physician. But that doesn't mean you can't encourage good sleep habits early on. Learning to fall asleep is a developmental milestone that you can begin to work on around 2 months *corrected* age.

QUIET

Before the WOO appears, a baby is more likely to fall asleep on the streets of downtown New York than in a remote part of a library. However, by about 2 months of age, when the sleep window is wide open, household noises tweak a sleeping baby's interest and may cause awakening from a light sleep state. The best way to avoid sleep interruptions is to use white noise to mask household noise.

RELAPSES

One of the most common complaints I hear is that a baby was sleeping through the night until sickness, a vacation, immunizations, or a new skill interfered. As I tell the families in my practice—if a baby forgets her good habits, she needs you to remind her!

ROLLING OVER

After months of insisting your baby sleep on his back, the time will come when you can no longer choose the position. Thank goodness this typically occurs as the incidence of SIDS is on the decline. Don't use pillows or positioning devices to force your baby into the back-to-sleep position. Once a baby can roll onto his side or tummy after being put to bed on his back, it's safe for him to sleep in any position he chooses. (Interestingly, many babies are rolling over later, around 7 months, now that they sleep on their backs.)

SIGN LANGUAGE

If your baby waves bye-bye or shakes his head no, he already uses sign language. Gestures are easy ways for babies to communicate. Baby sign language reduces guesswork and empowers a baby to express his needs directly. Even if you don't want to teach your baby a whole slew of words, consider at least teaching him "sleepy" and "bed."

To sign the word "sleepy": Put your fingers together and extend your thumb outward (hitchhiker's position). Turn your hand palm inward and flap your fingertips up and down in front of your eyes to express the drooping eyelids of a sleepy person.

To sign the word "bed": Lay your head down against your palm as if you were resting it on a pillow.

You can begin teaching anytime before he's picked up verbal speaking skills, but most babies lack the motor control to use sign language before 7 months. However, your baby will understand you before he starts to use signs himself. To learn more, visit the online sign dictionary at www.commtechlab.msu.edu/sites/aslweb/browser.htm or www.babyhandsproductions.com/index.aspx. Also, check out www.signingbaby.com, or pick up a copy of *Baby Signs: How to Talk with Your Baby Before Your Baby Can Talk,* by Linda Acredolo, Susan Goodwyn, and Douglas Abrams.

SLEEP STAGES

Sleep comes in two basic flavors: REM and non-REM sleep states.

- REM (RAPID EYE MOVEMENT SLEEP)
  The light sleep state in which dreams occur. Babies spend about 16 hours each day sleeping, and half of this is in REM sleep. Older children and adults not only sleep for fewer hours but spend much less time in REM sleep.
- NON-REM SLEEP
  Non-REM has four stages:

  - *Stage 1:* Drowsiness—eyes droop, may open and close; dozing
  - *Stage 2*: Light sleep—a baby may startle or jump with noise
  - *Stage 3*: Deep sleep—a baby is quiet and mostly still
  - *Stage 4*: Very deep sleep—a baby is quiet and does not move about

SLEEPWEAR

Every year, 200 to 300 burn injuries requiring emergency room treatment are the result of inappropriate sleepwear. Once a baby is mobile, loose-fitting pajamas and non-flame-retardant fabric pose a risk around open flames such as a candle or stove burner. National standards for sleepwear flammability for babies 9 months and older protect from burn injuries (before a baby is mobile, the risk of exposure to open flames is minimal). Sleepwear must be either flame resistant or fit snugly. Many organizations and experts feel these standards are too low and recommend flame-resistant fabric for all ages and fits. (*Note:* Follow laundry instructions carefully to maintain the flame-resistant property.)

SMOKING

Mothers who smoke during pregnancy put their babies at three times the risk for SIDS, and babies who breathe secondhand smoke are at $2\frac{1}{2}$ times the risk. Need I say more?

SOFA SLEEPING

Do not allow your baby to sleep on a regular or sleeper sofa, as this appears to increase the risk of SIDS.

SOLIDS

It would seem logical that a bedtime snack of cereal should help a baby sleep longer, but research suggests otherwise. In a study from Cleveland, 106 babies were divided into two groups—half got a bedtime feeding of cereal beginning at 5 weeks of age; the other half got bedtime cereal at 4 months. Parents kept sleep logs, and when researchers tallied the results, they found no significant improvement in sleep habits in either group. Actually, it just makes good sense: Babies wake up when they can't manage to fall back to sleep from a brief night awakening.

STUFFED ANIMALS

To reduce allergy triggers and SIDS risk, keep cribs free of stuffed animals and toys until your baby is able to roll over. Advise babysitters to do the same.

SWEATING

Many babies wake up each morning with soaking-wet hair. According to studies, one-third of babies sweat at night. Only a few health problems, such as apnea (see APNEA), cause night sweats. If your sweaty baby is growing and feeding well, it is extremely unlikely that there's an underlying health issue. Most likely the problem is that she's overdressed or overwrapped, or the bedroom is kept as warm as a sauna.

RED FLAGS: SEE YOUR DOCTOR IF YOUR BABY SWEATS AND:

- Has sleep apnea
- Isn't gaining adequate weight
- Breathes rapidly
- Feeds poorly
- Coughs daily and constantly

SWINGING CHAIRS

From June 2003 to June 2004, there were 140,000 baby swinging chairs recalled because of a safety hazard. Please check the Consumer Product Safety Commission Web site (www.cpsc. gov) before purchasing equipment for your baby, including items at garage sales, or accepting hand-me-downs from friends and family.

TEETHING

One of the most common mistakes parents make is blaming teething for close to everything, including sleep problems. Still, while many babies manage teething without pain, some suffer from sore gums. During the day, it may be easy for a baby to distract himself from the pain, but at night, alone in his crib, gum pain may be overwhelming. To relieve sore gums and salvage sleep, try counter pressure and cold. For instance, gently rub your baby's teeth with your finger or, better yet, something cold, like a frozen banana or cold washcloth. A chilled pacifier also works wonders. If these measures don't make your baby happier, you can use an analgesic.) Here are six signs your baby is teething (general speaking, four out of six of these signs will be present).

- BULGING GUMS. The outlines of teeth about to erupt are easily visible. The middle bottom teeth are usually the first place this happens.
- DROOLING. Your baby slobbers more than usual.
- FUSSING. Your baby is cranky and more difficult to comfort.
- NIGHT WAKING. Your baby is waking up at night and there seems to be no other explanation.
- BITING. Your baby gnaws on everything.
- A CHANGE IN FEEDING AND POOPING. Feeding and stool patterns may differ from usual. Some babies lose interest in solids, while others refuse to drink. Many parents report loose stools during teething.

Consult your physician if your baby is impossible to console or has a fever, and never tie a teething ring around a baby's neck.

TEMPERAMENT

Some babies are naturally better at falling and staying asleep than others are. Parents of easy babies make sleep learning look easy. On the flip side, some babies are exceptionally sensitive and moody, and sleep training them is treacherous. The important thing is to realize that a baby's temperament will influence whether she adapts readily or resists falling asleep every inch of the way. While we can't change a baby's temperament, we can learn to appreciate it and work with it.

TEMPERATURE (ROOM)

Babies are at an increased risk for SIDS when they get too hot. The room should be kept at 68° to 72°F. Do not overdress your baby or put a blanket over her head. Remember, if you're sweltering, so is your baby.

THUMB SUCKING

Although a pacifier should be used at bedtime, thumb sucking will help your baby sleep during the night. In my humble opinion, allowing a baby to suck his thumb enables him to manage his feelings and therefore sleep better, longer, and deeper.

TOP-OFFS

One of the best ways to reassure yourself that hunger is not causing your baby to wake up is to offer a top-off before you go to bed. Most babies are drowsy enough to be gently scooped out of bed or propped up and fed without fully waking up.

TWINS

Do not place more than one baby to sleep in a crib—ever.

UNDERSTIMULATION

New babies sleep better and longer when swaddled and surrounded with sound. Understimulation can literally drive them mad, like an itch they can't scratch.

VACATIONS

Planning ahead can help you and your baby avoid relapses. Think about sleeping arrangements, and ask yourself if holiday sleep situations will cause problems when you return home. You may not be able to make arrangements exactly as you'd like, but more thought and preparation beforehand will mean fewer relapses. Try to get back to your old ways as soon as you return.

WAITING

Many parents play the wait-and-see game without even realizing it. It goes something like this: "My baby was sleeping great until she got sick, and now, for the last 3 weeks, she's been waking up two or three times a night." Parents are busy waiting for their little pussycat to stop waking up, when, in fact, what she needs is for you to take charge.

WATER

Sometimes offering a bottle of water in place of warm milk puts a damper on night wakeups. It's as if a baby thinks, "What's the point of waking up if I only get water?"

WATER BED

Do not put your baby to bed in a water bed. The surface is too soft and can lead to suffocation if the baby rolls onto his tummy.

WHITE NOISE

Think of white noise as thousands of tones playing at once. The brain is overwhelmed with options and cannot single out a specific tone. Like camouflage, household noises are masked by white noise. Radio or TV static, vacuum cleaners, dishwashers, humidifiers, fans, and white-noise CDs are all wonderful sources.

WORK

Many babies relapse in sleep habits when Mom returns to work. They wake up frequently, as if to say, "Oh, Mommy, I miss you so much! We need more together time!" And many mommies feel so guilty that they decide the least they can do is get up with their little angel at night. Unfortunately, so begins the descent down the slippery no-sleep slope. But there is another option. When Mom returns to work, she should anticipate more wakeups and be prepared to give her baby extra reassurance, cuddles, and comfort as she lulls her baby to sleep.

YAWNING

The theory that we yawn because our bodies are trying to get rid of extra carbon dioxide and take in more oxygen seems to be in question. Humans do yawn, however, out of boredom and fatigue and because yawns are contagious. For the most part, babies yawn because they're tired. The moment you see your baby yawn, start the bedtime routine.

ZOMBIES

"I'm so tired I can barely think straight." If this describes you, sleep deprivation is clearly a problem. If you're sleep deprived, your baby is too! The Lull-a-Baby Sleep Plan can help you both get the sleep you need.

$\mathscr{I}$NDEX

Underscored page references indicate boxed text. **Boldface** references indicate illustrations.

C

Coping strategies, before opening
of WOO
avoiding sleep knots, 57–59
expecting 6-week peak, 55–56
partner involvement, 52–53
power naps, 49–51
raising baby's comfort level,
53–55
simplicity, 51–52
TLC technique, 56–57, **57**
Corn syrup, health risk from, 87
Cough syrups, 165
Crabbiness, from sleep deprivation,
17–19
Cradles, rocking, 173
Crib
associated with sleep by older
baby, 139
elevating, for colds, 164, 172
orientation of, after moving,
180
positioning baby into, 99
safety considerations for, 98,
167–68
twins and, 189
Crib blox, 172
Crib mobile, 172, 180
Crying
in older babies, 149, 150–51
quieting, 121, 123
with Gentle Tough Plan,
147–48, 151
with H.E.L.P. technique,
141–45
with Sleep fix, 148–49, 151
with Stop, Look, and Listen
technique, 104–5, 107, 121
with TLC technique, 56–57, **57**,
107–8
with WOW technique, 81–91
reading meaning of, 105, 107, 107,
168
at 6-week peak, 55–56
sleep myth about, 20

Cry-it-out strategy, 23, 24–25, 26, 29
unnecessary in Lull-a-Baby Sleep
Plan, xviii, 77, 78
when to use, 26
Cuddling, 9
in TLC technique, 7, 56, **57**, 108

D

Day/night confusion, 132, 168
Decongestants, 165
Dehydration, 169
Dental problems, from pacifiers,
86–87
Depression, postpartum, 17, 158–59
Depression After Delivery, 159
Diapers, 169
Dimmers, 172–73

E

Ear infections, 87, 166, 169, 179
Empathize, in H.E.L.P. for older
baby, 141–44
Even-tempered babies, cry-it-out
strategy for, 24, 25, **25**
Eyes rolling back, 170

F

Fade Away, for parents, 152–53, 152
Family-bed sleep philosophy, 23,
25–27, 54. *See also* Bed
sharing
Fathers, encouraging involvement
of, 52–53, 108
Fatigue, from sleep deprivation.
See Sleep deprivation

Older baby
definition of, 6
frustration in, as motivation for
change, 136, 152
pushing sleep button of, 138–40
skills of, 136–38
sleep glitches with, 149–51
undoing bad sleep habits of, 20,
140–49
"Oops, I'll Be Right Back" routine,
144–45, 148, 151, 152, 153
Optimism, importance of, 64
Oral ease. See also Pacifiers;
Thumb sucking
in WOW bedtime regimen, 81,
84–87
Overheating, 91, 120, 186–87
Overtiredness, as sleep obstacle,
38, 118, 131–32

P

Pacifiers
choosing, 86, 181–82
dependency on, as sleep
mistake, 41–42, 117
drawbacks of, 85
origin of, 85
proper use of, 54, 58, 85–87,
117–18, 120
for reducing SIDS, 9, 42, 85, 117,
118
safety considerations for, 182
with TLC technique, 56
Persevere, in H.E.L.P. for older
baby, 145
Pets, 182
Picking up baby, when charming
baby to sleep, 107, 108, 110
Pillows, 167, 182, 183
Poor sleepers, sleep myth about,
20

Positional devices, 173, 182, 183
Postpartum depression, 17, 158–59
Postpartum psychosis, 158
Postpartum Support International,
159
Power naps, for parents, 49–51, 64,
126, 132–33
Premature babies, 182–83
Props. See also Pacifiers
sleep problems from, 120
Psychological effects of crying,
sleep myth about, 20

Q

Quiet, 183

R

Raw-nose relief, 166
Reading, as calming technique, 104,
106
Relapses in sleep habits, 163,
175–76, 183, 189, 190
Relaxation response, 71
REM (rapid eye movement) sleep,
4, 5, 8, 10, 185
Rocking cradle, 173
Rocking to sleep, problems with,
32, 33, 36, 37, 59
Rolling over, 183
Room sharing, 95, 119

S

Schedule, encouraging, 121–23
Secondhand items, safety of, 175,
187

Voice. *See also* Talking
    as calming technique, 102–4, **103**,
        106, 108
Volatile babies, cry-it-out strategy
    for, 24–25, **25**

W

Waiting, for sleep training, 42–43,
    189–90
Water beds, 96, 190
Water feedings, 190
Web site, for Lull-a-baby support
    and motivation, 155
Weight gain, from sleep
    deprivation, 17
Weissbluth, Marc, 35
White noise
    as conducive to sleep, 34, 54,
        170, 190
    for naps, 126, 129
    questions about, 83
    in shared room, 119
    sources of, 166–67, 190
    when to use, 95, 120, 183
    in WOW bedtime regimen, 81, 82,
        84
Window of Opportunity (WOO)
    closing of, 5, 7, 11, 14, 135
    common questions about,
        77–80
    definition of, xvi, 7
    for fixing sleep problems, 151

missing, xix, 43, 76–78, 135
napping during, 118
opening of, 4, 10, 11, 36, 56, 59,
    105, 107, 163, 168, 173, 180,
    183
    coping strategies before,
        47–59
    sleep deprivation before, 47
    taking advantage of, 72–73, 113
purpose of, xviii, **xviii**
sleep needs during, 118
sleep results with, xvii, 113
timeline of, xvi, 4, 5, 6, 73–76,
    78–79
WOO. *See* Window of Opportunity
Work return, sleep relapses from,
    190
WOW bedtime regimen, 81–91
Wrap. *See also* Swaddling
    in WOW bedtime regimen, 81,
        87–91

Y

Yawning, 38, 171, 190–91
Younger baby, definition of, 6

Z

Zip-around safety blanket, 173
Zombies, 191